a cook's guide

a cook's guide

Copyright © Donna Hay 2011. Design copyright © Donna Hay 2011
Editor-in-chief: Donna Hay
Art direction and design: Genevieve McKelvey, Hayley Incoll and Zoë Doyle
Copy editors: Melanie Hansche and Lara Picone
Recipes and styling: Donna Hay, Steve Pearce, Justine Poole
Additional recipes and styling: Kate Murdoch, Jane Collings, Kirsten Jenkins, Siobhan Boyle

Reproduction by Graphic Print Group, South Australia
Produced in China by RR Donnelley on 157gsm Chinese Matt Art
5 4 3 2 1   11 12 13 14

Fourth Estate
An imprint of HarperCollins*Publishers*

First published in Australia and New Zealand in 2011,
by Fourth Estate, an imprint of HarperCollins*Publishers*

Published in Canada by HarperCollins Publishers Ltd
First Canadian edition

HarperCollins*Publishers* Australia Pty Limited, Level 13, 201 Elizabeth Street,
Sydney, NSW 2000, Australia. ABN 36 009 913 517
HarperCollins*Publishers*, 31 View Road, Glenfield,
Auckland 10, New Zealand

Library and Archives Canada Cataloguing in Publication information is available upon request.
ISBN: 9781443411059

on the cover
Front, L–R: Shortcrust pastry, page 80, Chris Court. Chilli and fennel roasted pork belly, page 13, Chris Court. One-pan
chorizo, olive and feta polenta, page 30, William Meppem. Caramel slice, page 84, William Meppem. Three cheese frittata,
page 64, Chris Court. Creamed corn polenta with crispy skin chicken, page 30, William Meppem. Back, L–R: Coconut and
lemon curd tarts, page 82, Chris Court. Baked risotto, page 34, Chris Court. Chocolate, William Meppem. Scones, page 86,
William Meppem. Choux pastry, page 90, Vanessa Levis. Chocolate crème caramels, page 125, William Meppem.

Photographs copyright 2011 © Chris Court pages 5, 8, 9, 11–13, 15–19, 26, 34–40, 44, 46, 47, 49, 50, 53,
56–59, 64, 65, 67–71, 72–75, 77, 80–83, 85, 95–101, 102, 103, 105–112, 114, 116, 117, 119, 126–127. © William Meppem
pages 4–7, 20, 26–29, 31, 42–43, 45, 46, 48, 54, 55, 72–73, 79, 84, 86–88, 101, 122–127, 134–136. © Con Poulos pages 20,
45, 49, 79, 94, 115, 121. © Vanessa Levis pages 22–24, 60–62, 90, 91, 93. © Ben Dearnley pages 21, 120. © Andy Lewis
pages 14, 33. © Luke Burgess page 32. © Tanya Zouev page 78. © Jonny Valiant page 121.

donna hay

a cook's guide

the best of donna hay magazine's how to cook

HarperCollins*Publishers*Ltd

contents

* Ingredients marked with an asterisk
have a glossary entry

Like my grandmother and my mother (and most other home cooks out there), I had a definitive cookbook that was my go-to guide for basic recipes and techniques. Like how to roast a chicken, make lump-free gravy or bake the perfect sponge cake. This book came about with the same intention, to create a handy resource for all the essentials.

a cook's guide is a compilation of all the very best How To Cook columns that have appeared in donna hay magazine over the last 10 years. They are classic recipes we think should be in every cook's arsenal, in a detailed step-by-step format with photographs. We've covered everything from classic roast dinners and essential sauces to your favourite baked treats and timeless desserts.

So whether you're learning to cook or would just like a good handle on the classics in one easy book, this is your one-stop cook's guide. Happy cooking!

Donna

mains

roast lamb

roast pork

pork crackling

perfect steak

roast beef

corned beef

roast chicken

butterfly chicken

chicken soup

poaching chicken

chicken salad

polenta

gratin

filleting fish

baked risotto

gnocchi

roast lamb

The savoury aroma of a lamb roast is enough to have mouths watering before the table is even set. Succulent and versatile, this classic will win hearts every time.

step 1

step 2

roast lamb with rosemary and garlic

1 lamb leg, trimmed
2 bunches rosemary
2 heads garlic, halved
olive oil, for rubbing
sea salt flakes

before you begin

serving sizes
+ up to 4 people, you will need a 1.75–2kg leg of lamb
+ up to 6 people, 2–2.5kg
+ up to 8 people, over 2.5kg

cooking times (for medium-well done)
+ traditional lamb leg, roast for 18 minutes per 500g
+ butterflied lamb leg, roast for 10 minutes per 500g
+ tunnel-boned lamb leg, roast for 20 minutes per 500g
+ easy-carve lamb leg, roast for 18 minutes per 500g

Step 1 Preheat oven to 200°C (400°F). Weigh the lamb to determine the cooking time (see *before you begin*, left).

Step 2 Place the rosemary and garlic in a baking dish lined with non-stick baking paper and top with the lamb. Rub the lamb with oil and sprinkle with salt.

Step 3 Roast for the calculated cooking time or until cooked to your liking. Allow to stand for 10 minutes before carving. Serve with mint sauce (see recipe, right).

serve with...
MINT SAUCE
Place ½ cup (125ml) apple juice, ¼ cup (60ml) water, 1 tablespoon wholegrain mustard and 1 tablespoon white wine vinegar in a saucepan over medium heat. Bring to the boil, reduce heat to low and simmer for 3 minutes. Remove from heat, stir through ⅓ cup shredded mint and allow to stand for 5 minutes. *Makes approx. ¾ cup (180ml).*

quince-glazed lamb

1 lamb leg, trimmed
⅓ cup (80ml) orange juice
2 tablespoons quince paste*
2 teaspoons Dijon mustard
2 teaspoons olive oil
sea salt and cracked black pepper

Preheat oven to 200°C (400°F). Weigh the lamb to determine the cooking time (see *before you begin*, page 8). Place the lamb on a rack in a baking dish. Roast for ¾ of the calculated cooking time.

While the lamb is roasting, place the orange juice, quince paste, mustard, oil, salt and pepper in a small saucepan over low heat. Stir until the quince paste is dissolved. Increase heat to medium and simmer for 2 minutes.

Brush the lamb with the glaze. Return to the oven and roast, brushing at 5-minute intervals, for the remaining cooking time or until cooked to your liking. Brush with any remaining glaze. Allow to stand for 10 minutes before carving. Serve with roasted vegetables, if desired.

herb-marinated lamb

1 butterflied lamb leg⁺, trimmed
½ cup (125ml) olive oil
⅓ cup (80ml) red wine
sea salt and cracked black pepper
¼ cup chopped oregano leaves
¼ cup chopped flat-leaf parsley leaves
2 cloves garlic, finely chopped
3 brown onions, cut into thick wedges

Weigh the lamb to determine the cooking time (see *before you begin*, page 8). Place the oil, wine, salt, pepper, oregano, parsley and garlic in a bowl and mix to combine. Place the lamb in a non-metallic dish and pour over the marinade, turning to coat. Cover with plastic wrap and place in the fridge for 3 hours or overnight.

Preheat oven to 200°C (400°F). Remove the lamb from the marinade. Place the onions in a baking dish and top with the lamb. Roast for the calculated cooking time, basting regularly with the pan juices, or until cooked to your liking. Allow to stand for 10 minutes before carving. Serve with the onions.
+ *This cut has had all the bones removed before being opened to become one large flat piece, making it quicker to cook. It is perfect for marinating. Make shallow cuts to the fatty side of the meat before marinating for several hours or overnight.*

thyme and lemon stuffed lamb

1 easy-carve lamb leg⁺, trimmed
2 cloves garlic, sliced
1½ tablespoons shredded lemon zest
½ bunch thyme sprigs
sea salt and cracked black pepper
olive oil, for rubbing

Preheat oven to 200°C (400°F). Weigh the lamb to determine the cooking time (see *before you begin*, page 8). Open out the lamb and fill with the garlic, lemon zest, thyme, salt and pepper. Roll to enclose and tie with kitchen string⁺⁺. Place the lamb on a rack in a baking dish, rub with oil and sprinkle with salt. Roast for the calculated cooking time or until cooked to your liking. Allow to stand for 10 minutes before carving.
+ *This cut of lamb is popular because all the bones, except the end leg shank, have been removed, giving you something to hold on to when carving.*
++ *See technique for tying roast beef, page 15. Tie the string firmly as the meat will shrink as it cooks, causing the string to loosen.*

sage and parmesan stuffed lamb

1 tunnel-boned lamb leg⁺, trimmed
1¾ cups (115g) fresh breadcrumbs
1 tablespoon finely grated lemon rind
¼ cup shredded sage leaves
¼ cup (20g) finely grated parmesan
20g butter, softened
sea salt and cracked black pepper
olive oil, for rubbing

Preheat oven to 200°C (400°F). Weigh the lamb to determine the cooking time (see *before you begin*, page 8). Place the breadcrumbs, lemon rind, sage, parmesan, butter, salt and pepper in a bowl and mix to combine. Fill the tunnel hole of the lamb with the stuffing mixture and roll to enclose. Tie the lamb with kitchen string (see tip, above), making sure you enclose all the stuffing. Place the lamb on a rack in a baking dish, rub with oil and sprinkle with salt and pepper. Roast for the calculated cooking time or until cooked to your liking. Allow to stand for 10 minutes before carving. Serve with steamed greens, if desired.
+ *This cut is the same shape as a traditional lamb leg but without the bones. After the leg bones are removed, a tunnel is left through the meat, which makes it easy to stuff. Make sure you tie your lamb once it has been stuffed to ensure the stuffing doesn't fall out.*

quince-glazed lamb

thyme and lemon stuffed lamb

herb-marinated lamb

sage and parmesan stuffed lamb

roast pork

Sweet and juicy roast pork encased in a crispy crackle is a lip-smacking family favourite that's guaranteed to inspire a second round of helpings.

step 2

step 3

roast pork

3kg boneless pork loin, trimmed
1 x quantity stuffing (see recipes, right)
olive oil and sea salt flakes, for rubbing
1 head garlic, halved

recipe notes

To make room for the stuffing in a boneless loin of pork, you need to use a sharp knife to separate and cut away the small fillet and any excess meat from around the loin. Alternatively, ask your butcher to do this for you.

step 1 Using the point of a sharp knife, score the skin of the pork at 1cm intervals. (Follow the pork crackling technique, opposite page, for perfect crackling.)

step 2 Preheat oven to 220°C (425°F). Remove the fillet and any excess meat from around the loin of pork. Use a knife to separate the skin from the loin, leaving 3cm joined. Place the stuffing down the centre.

step 3 Roll the loin over the stuffing and secure with kitchen string. Rub the skin with oil and salt.

step 4 Place pork and garlic on a lightly greased rack in a baking dish and roast for 20 minutes. Reduce heat to 200°C (400°F) and roast for a further 50-55 minutes or until pork is cooked to your liking. Allow to rest for 5 minutes. Remove string and slice. *Serves 8.*

try this...

THYME AND ONION STUFFING
Place 1 tablespoon oil and 120g butter in a frying pan over medium heat. Add 4 sliced onions and cook, stirring occasionally, for 10-15 minutes or until onion is softened. Remove from heat and add 2 tablespoons thyme leaves and 4 cups (280g) fresh breadcrumbs.

PEAR AND SAGE STUFFING
Place 1 sliced brown pear, 2 tablespoons chopped sage, 1 tablespoon brown sugar, 15g softened butter, 1 teaspoon cracked black pepper and sea salt flakes in a bowl and toss to combine. Place the coated pears down the centre of the pork.

pork crackling

You will need:
a small, sharp knife
sea salt flakes
olive oil

step 1 Using a small sharp knife, score the skin at 1cm intervals.

step 2 Rub the skin with salt and refrigerate, uncovered, overnight. This will draw the moisture out of the skin and produce a better crackling.

step 3 Preheat oven to 220°C (425°F). Brush the salt from the skin and pat dry with absorbent paper to remove any excess moisture. Brush the skin with oil and rub with more salt, making sure to rub into the cuts. Place the pork, skin-side up, in a roasting tray and roast for 20-30 minutes or until skin has crackled. Reduce heat to 200°C (400°F) and proceed with your recipe. If using a pork loin, tie the roast with kitchen string.

Tip: The best cuts to use for pork crackling are those with the skin left on and a large surface area for crackling, such as rolled pork loin, bone-in pork shoulder or leg and pork belly.

chilli and fennel roasted pork belly

1.2kg pork belly, bones removed
olive oil, for brushing
sea salt flakes
1 tablespoon dried chilli flakes
1 tablespoon fennel seeds
8 small pears, halved

Prepare the pork following steps 1-2. Preheat oven to 180°C (350°F). Brush the salt from the skin and pat dry with absorbent paper to remove any excess moisture. Brush the skin with oil and rub with salt, chilli and the fennel, making sure to rub into the cuts. Place the pork, skin-side down, in a roasting tray and roast for 1 hour. Turn the pork and roast for a further 1 hour or until the skin is golden and crunchy. Brush the pears with oil and add to the tray in the final 20-25 minutes of cooking. Serve the pork with the pears, steamed green beans and a shaved fennel salad, if desired. Serves 8.

step 1

step 2

perfect steak

You will need:
a large non-stick frying pan
cooking tongs
aluminium foil

step 1 Bring 4 x 200g sirloin steaks (3cm-thick) to room temperature. Brush with olive oil and sprinkle with sea salt and cracked black pepper.

step 2 Heat a large non-stick frying pan over high heat until hot. Cook the steaks, 2 at a time, to your liking using the cooking times (below left) as a guide. Turn each steak only once using tongs.

step 3 Place the steaks on a plate and cover with aluminium foil. Allow to rest for 5 minutes before serving. Serve with your favourite sides.

Tip: Our cooking times (below left) are based on 3cm-thick steaks, cooked in a frying pan. Shorten the times slightly when using a char-grill pan or barbecue, as they retain more heat. You can ask your butcher to cut your steaks to the desired size.

steak with chilli, lime and garlic butter

100g butter, softened
1 long red chilli, seeded and finely chopped
1 tablespoon shredded lime zest
1 clove garlic, crushed
4 x 200g sirloin steaks (3cm-thick)
200g blanched green beans, to serve

Place the butter, chilli, lime zest and garlic in a bowl and mix to combine. Place the butter mixture in the centre of a sheet of non-stick baking paper and roll to form a log. Twist ends to seal and refrigerate until firm.

Cook the steaks to your liking following steps 1–3. Top steaks with slices of the butter and serve with the green beans. *Serves 4.*

step 1   step 2

cooking times

rare	2 minutes each side
medium-rare	$3\frac{1}{2}$ minutes each side
medium	4 minutes each side
medium-well	$4\frac{1}{2}$ minutes each side
well done	5 minutes each side

roast beef

Tying a beef roast will keep everything in place while the meat becomes succulent and tender. And, best of all, leftovers make delicious sandwiches the next day.

step 2   step 3

You will need:
a small, sharp knife
kitchen scissors
kitchen string

step 1 Using a small, sharp knife, trim any excess fat and sinew from the beef.

step 2 Cut a metre-long piece of kitchen string. Starting at the end of the beef furthest from you, secure the string in the centre at the top of the beef with a knot, leaving a little 'tail' of string about 10cm long.

step 3 Pull the long end of the string down from the knot. At about 2cm, use your finger to create a hook in the string. Holding the string in place with your finger, wrap the tail of the string around the beef, bringing it back to your finger, before threading it through the hook. Pull the string down from the hook to create another 2cm section. Repeat along the length of the beef at 2cm intervals.

step 4 Once at the end, take the string under the beef, weave through the strings on the underside and secure to the tail of string at the top where you started.

prosciutto-wrapped roast beef

1kg beef scotch fillet, trimmed
olive oil, for brushing
sea salt and cracked black pepper
12 slices prosciutto
¼ cup (75g) store-bought caramelised onion relish (or see recipe, page 46)

Preheat oven to 180°C (350°F). Brush beef with oil and sprinkle with salt and pepper. Heat a large frying pan over high heat. Cook beef for 1–2 minutes each side or until browned. Set aside. Arrange the prosciutto slices on a cutting board, making sure they overlap. Top prosciutto with the caramelised onion. Place the beef in the middle of the prosciutto and fold over to enclose. Secure with kitchen string. Place on a baking tray, brush with oil and roast for 50–55 minutes for medium-rare or until cooked to your liking. Allow to rest for 5 minutes before slicing. *Serves 4–6.*

corned beef

This traditional recipe refers to the method of preserving meat using salt and is still a favourite today. See our spin on serving it for a new repertoire of cool-weather classics.

step 1

step 2

corned beef

1.5kg corned silverside or brisket
3 bay leaves
12 peppercorns
6 cloves
⅓ cup (80ml) malt vinegar
½ cup (90g) brown sugar
6 pickling onions, peeled
1 bunch baby carrots, trimmed and peeled

step 1 Place the beef in a large, heavy-based deep saucepan. Add the bay leaves, peppercorns, cloves, vinegar, sugar, onions and enough water to cover. Place over high heat and bring to the boil.

step 2 Reduce the heat to low, cover and simmer for 1 hour 30 minutes or until the beef is firm to the touch. Add the carrots in the last 5 minutes of cooking. Use a slotted spoon to occasionally skim the foam from the surface. *Serves 6.*

tips + tricks

KEEP IT COVERED
It's important to keep the beef submerged in liquid during cooking. Top up the saucepan with boiling water, if required.

DELICIOUS SERVES
For the most tender slices, slice corned beef across the grain. Toss in a salad of roasted vegies and autumnal bitter greens or for a traditional take, serve with white sauce – just add parsley, chives or green onion (scallion) to freshen it up. Store any leftovers, whole, in the cooking liquid and covered, in the fridge for up to 3 days.

A LITTLE SPICE
Experiment with other spices and herbs, such as cinnamon, star anise, thyme, parsley or whole garlic cloves; simply add to the pot at step 1.

recipe notes

The general cooking time for corned beef is 25-30 minutes per 500g. You can tell the beef is ready when it's firm to the touch like a medium steak, and when an inserted skewer comes out easily.

new york deli sandwich

12 slices rye bread
softened butter, for spreading
1 cup (300g) whole-egg mayonnaise
1 tablespoon hot English mustard
1 x quantity corned beef (see recipe, page 16)
12 slices Swiss cheese
dill pickles (gherkins), to serve
caramelised cabbage
30g butter
300g white cabbage, shredded
¼ cup (55g) caster (superfine) sugar
¼ cup (60ml) malt vinegar

To make the caramelised cabbage, place the butter in a saucepan over high heat. Add the cabbage and cook, stirring, for 5 minutes or until softened. Add the sugar and the vinegar and cook, stirring, for 10 minutes or until most of the liquid is evaporated and the cabbage is tender. Set aside.

Spread the bread with butter on one side and mayonnaise and mustard on the other side. Slice the corned beef and place on half the bread slices, butter-side down. Top with cheese and cabbage and sandwich with remaining slices. Heat a large non-stick frying pan over high heat. Cook the sandwiches, in batches, for 2–3 minutes each side, turning carefully, or until golden and the cheese is melted. Serve with the dill pickles. *Makes 6.*

corned beef in broth with salsa verde

1 x quantity corned beef (see recipe, page 16)
salsa verde
1 tablespoon salted capers, rinsed
⅓ cup mint leaves
⅓ cup flat-leaf parsley leaves
2 anchovy fillets
1 clove garlic, crushed
½ cup (125ml) extra-virgin olive oil

To make the salsa verde, roughly chop the capers, mint, parsley and anchovies. Place in a bowl with the garlic and oil and stir to combine. Set aside.

Slice the beef into 12 thick slices and place into serving bowls with the carrots and onions. Ladle over the broth and top with salsa verde to serve. *Serves 6.*

corned beef pies

40g butter
2 tablespoons plain (all-purpose) flour
⅔ cup (160ml) chicken stock
1¼ cups (310ml) milk
1 x quantity corned beef (see recipe, page 16)
1 cup (120g) frozen peas
2 tablespoons chopped flat-leaf parsley leaves
1 sheet store-bought puff pastry, thawed
1 egg, lightly beaten

Preheat oven to 200°C (400°F). Melt the butter in a saucepan over low heat. Add the flour and cook, stirring, for 5–7 minutes or until golden and sandy in texture. Gradually whisk in the stock and milk, increase the heat to medium and cook for a further 5 minutes or until thickened. Add 400g shredded corned beef, the chopped carrots and half the onions, peas and parsley and stir to combine. Spoon into 4 x 1 cup-capacity (250ml) ovenproof dishes and place on a baking tray. Cut the pastry into 4 x 10cm rounds and place over the pies. Brush with egg. Top with remaining onions and bake for 20 minutes or until puffed and golden. *Makes 4.*

corned beef hash

500g sebago (starchy) potatoes, peeled and grated
1 x quantity corned beef (see recipe, page 16)
2 eggs, lightly beaten
2 green onions (scallions), sliced
1 tablespoon store-bought grated horseradish*
sea salt and cracked black pepper
2 tablespoons olive oil
20g butter
tomato salsa
2 vine-ripened tomatoes, chopped
½ cup flat-leaf parsley leaves
1 tablespoon red wine vinegar
sea salt and cracked black pepper

To make the tomato salsa, place the tomato, parsley, vinegar, salt and pepper in a bowl and mix to combine. Set aside.

Squeeze the grated potato to remove any excess water and pat dry. Shred 250g corned beef and place in a bowl with the potato, egg, green onion, horseradish, salt and pepper and mix well to combine. Heat the oil and butter in a large non-stick frying pan over high heat. Cook ½ cupfuls of the mixture, pressing to flatten, for 4 minutes each side or until golden and crisp. Drain on absorbent paper. Serve with the salsa. *Makes 8.*

roast chicken

Plump, juicy and filled with a delicious, herby stuffing, a perfectly cooked chicken is guaranteed to lure everyone to the table with its tempting aroma.

step 1

step 2

roast chicken

1 x 1.6kg chicken
1 x quantity stuffing (see recipes, right)
olive oil, for brushing
sea salt flakes, for sprinkling
water or chicken stock

cooking times

Roast a whole chicken in a preheated 190°C (375°F) oven according to this chart.

size	weight	time
14	1.4kg	50-55 min.
16	1.6kg	1 hour
18	1.8kg	65-70 min.

step 1 Preheat oven to 190°C (375°F). Wash the chicken and pat dry with absorbent paper. Spoon the stuffing loosely into the cavity of the chicken. If the stuffing is packed too tightly, it won't heat all the way through.

step 2 Tie the legs of the chicken together with kitchen string, making sure the legs are almost touching. This will help to keep the shape of the chicken while it roasts, and will also prevent the stuffing from coming out of the cavity.

step 3 Place the chicken on a lightly greased rack in a roasting pan. Brush with oil and sprinkle with salt. Pour the water or chicken stock into the base of the pan (the steam will help the chicken to cook evenly and the pan juices are a great base for a gravy). Roast for 1 hour or until cooked through and the juices run clear when tested with a skewer.

try this...

HERB STUFFING

Heat 2 teaspoons oil in a frying pan over medium heat. Add 1 small finely chopped onion and cook for 5 minutes or until golden. Place in a bowl with 3 cups (210g) fresh breadcrumbs, 1½ teaspoons chopped fresh herbs (thyme, rosemary or sage), 30g softened butter, sea salt and cracked black pepper and mix well to combine.

PARMESAN, PINE NUT AND PARSLEY STUFFING

Place 3 cups (210g) fresh breadcrumbs, ⅓ cup (25g) finely grated parmesan, 3 tablespoons toasted pine nuts, ¼ cup chopped flat-leaf parsley, 20g softened butter, sea salt and cracked black pepper in a bowl and mix well to combine.

butterfly chicken

You will need:
kitchen scissors or chicken shears
a cutting board

step 1 Position the chicken breast-side down, so the back is facing up and the drumsticks are facing towards you. Using sharp kitchen scissors or chicken shears, cut closely along either side of the backbone and remove.

step 2 Turn chicken breast-side up and press down firmly on breastbone to flatten chicken. Tuck the wings under before roasting.

spice-roasted chicken

1 teaspoon dried chilli flakes
3 cloves garlic, crushed
½ teaspoon smoked paprika*
1 teaspoon dried oregano leaves
1 tablespoon shredded lemon zest
¼ cup (60ml) red wine vinegar
¼ cup (60ml) olive oil
sea salt and cracked black pepper
1 x 1.6kg whole chicken, butterflied

Preheat oven to 200°C (400°F). Place the chilli, garlic, paprika, oregano, lemon zest, vinegar, oil, salt and pepper in a bowl and mix well to combine. Place the chicken on a baking tray lined with non-stick baking paper, pour over the chilli mixture and spread over chicken to coat. Roast for 45 minutes, brushing with the pan juices halfway through, or until cooked through and golden. *Serves 4.*

step 1   step 2

cooking times

These times are based on roasting an average 1.6kg chicken.

breast fillet (bone in)	20 minutes
maryland	30 minutes
butterflied	45 minutes

chicken soup

With its soothing and wholesome flavour, it's little wonder this nostalgic dish is said to be good for the soul. Make it your own and pass the recipe down just as grandma did.

basic chicken soup

2 stalks celery, chopped
1 carrot, peeled and chopped
1 cup (220g) risoni or small pasta
sea salt and cracked black pepper
chopped flat-leaf parsley leaves, to serve
chicken stock
1 x 1.5kg chicken
1 brown onion, chopped
2 cloves garlic, chopped
2 stalks celery, chopped
1 carrot, peeled and chopped
4 bay leaves
1 teaspoon black peppercorns
2.5 litres water or enough to cover

step 1

step 2

step 1 To make the chicken stock, place the chicken, onion, garlic, celery, carrot, bay leaves, peppercorns and water in a large saucepan over high heat.

step 2 Bring to the boil, cover and reduce the heat to low. Cook for 1 hour or until the chicken is cooked through. Use a metal spoon to occasionally skim the foam from the surface⁺.

step 3 Remove chicken from the stock and cool slightly. Remove the skin and discard. Shred the chicken meat from the bones

(see *cook's tip*, below) and set aside. Strain the stock, discarding vegetables.

step 4 Return the stock to the pan with the celery, carrot, risoni, shredded chicken and salt and pepper. Cook over high heat for 10–15 minutes or until the vegetables are tender. Top with parsley to serve. *Serves 6.*

+ *Skimming the foam from the surface of the soup will result in a nice, clear broth with a cleaner and sweeter flavour.*

cook's tip

To shred the meat, place the chicken on a board and hold firmly (you may need to use tongs if it is still hot). Peel away the skin and use a fork to shred the meat from the bone. Follow the grain of the meat so it comes away in long strands.

tomato, chicken and bean soup

lemony chicken and rice soup

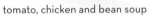

creamy mushroom and chicken soup

ginger chicken soup with asian greens

lemony chicken and rice soup

1 x quantity chicken stock and chicken (see recipe, page 22)
1 cup (200g) medium-grain rice
1 tablespoon shredded lemon zest
sea salt and cracked black pepper
1 tablespoon lemon juice
½ cup mint leaves, to serve

Place the strained stock, rice, lemon zest, salt and pepper in a large saucepan over medium heat. Bring to the boil and cook for 20–25 minutes or until the rice is al dente. Add the shredded chicken and lemon juice and cook for 1 minute or until chicken is warmed through. Sprinkle with mint to serve. *Serves 6.*

creamy mushroom and chicken soup

¼ cup (60ml) olive oil
2 leeks, sliced
400g Swiss brown mushrooms, sliced
700g sebago (starchy) potatoes, peeled and chopped
2 tablespoons thyme leaves
½ cup (125ml) dry white wine
1 x quantity chicken stock and chicken (see recipe, page 22)
1 cup (250ml) single (pouring) cream
sea salt and cracked black pepper
sour cream and thyme leaves, extra, to serve

Heat the oil in a large saucepan over medium heat. Add the leek, mushroom, potato and thyme and cook for 10 minutes or until browned. Add wine and cook for 1 minute. Add the strained stock, bring to the boil and cook for 10 minutes or until the potato is tender. Process in a blender, in batches, until smooth. Return to the pan, add the cream, shredded chicken, salt and pepper and cook over high heat for 1 minute or until the chicken is warmed through. Top with sour cream and extra thyme to serve. *Serves 6.*

tomato, chicken and bean soup

2 tablespoons olive oil
3 rashers bacon, rind removed and chopped
½ teaspoon dried chilli flakes
1 x quantity chicken stock and chicken (see recipe, page 22)
1 x 400g can chopped tomatoes
100g macaroni or small pasta
sea salt and cracked black pepper
2 x 400g cans white (cannellini) beans, rinsed and drained
250g green beans, trimmed and sliced
½ cup (40g) finely grated parmesan, to serve

Heat the oil in a large saucepan over high heat. Add the bacon and chilli and cook for 2–3 minutes or until browned. Add the strained stock, shredded chicken, tomatoes, pasta, salt and pepper and cook for 8–10 minutes. Add the white beans and green beans and cook for 1 minute. Top with parmesan to serve. *Serves 6.*

ginger chicken soup with asian greens

1 x quantity chicken stock and chicken (see recipe, page 22)
50g ginger, peeled and thinly sliced
2 green onions (scallions), sliced
4 small red chillies, halved
¼ cup (60ml) soy sauce
½ teaspoon sesame oil
2 tablespoons Chinese rice wine (Shaoxing)*
2 bunches baby bok choy, quartered
coriander (cilantro) leaves, to serve

Place the strained chicken stock, ginger, half of the green onions, chilli, soy, sesame oil and rice wine in a large saucepan over high heat. Bring to the boil and cook for 5 minutes. Add the bok choy and shredded chicken and cook for a further 3–5 minutes or until the bok choy is tender. Top with remaining green onion and coriander to serve. *Serves 6.*

poaching chicken

You will need:
1 lemon, sliced
1 sprig flat-leaf parsley
black peppercorns, roughly crushed
4 x 150g chicken breast fillets, trimmed

step 1 Fill a large, deep frying pan with water and add the lemon, parsley and peppercorns. Bring the water to the boil. Reduce the heat and simmer for 2–3 minutes.

step 2 Add the chicken, making sure it is covered with the poaching liquid. Cook for 8 minutes. Remove from the heat and allow to stand in the poaching liquid for 15 minutes. Remove chicken from the pan and serve hot, or keep in the fridge until ready to serve. *Serves 4.*

tips + tricks

SLOW AND STEADY
The first rule of poaching is to keep it low and slow. Turn down the heat and keep the liquid at a steady simmer. Poach a 150g chicken breast fillet for 8 minutes and allow to stand in the poaching liquid for 15 minutes. Remove the chicken from the liquid and stand for a further 5 minutes before shredding or slicing. A larger fillet (up to 200g) will need to stand for a further 5–10 minutes in the liquid.

READY OR NOT
To test if the chicken is cooked through, press the thickest part of the breast with tongs. It should feel firm and springy. Poached chicken can be stored in the refrigerator for up to 3 days.

EXTRA FLAVOUR
Try adding other flavours to your poaching liquid, such as ginger or garlic, dill, thyme and lemon thyme for fresh-tasting results. Or, for Asian-inspired flavour, you can use kaffir lime leaves, coriander (cilantro), lemongrass or chilli.

SERVING IDEAS
Poached chicken is delicious sliced or shredded and added to salads, sandwiches, pastas, frittatas and soups.

step 1   step 2

chicken salad

Packed-full of fresh flavour, succulent chicken and creamy egg, you can serve this tasty, must-know salad with crusty bread for a substantial lunch or dinner.

step 1

step 2

chicken, egg and lettuce salad

4 eggs
1.2kg store-bought barbecued chicken, skin off, shredded
2 baby cos (romaine) lettuces, leaves separated
4 pickled onions, thinly sliced
¼ cup chopped chives
buttermilk dressing
½ cup (125ml) buttermilk
1 tablespoon lemon juice
sea salt and cracked black pepper

step 1 To make the buttermilk dressing, place buttermilk, lemon juice, salt and pepper in a bowl and whisk until well combined. Set aside.

step 2 Cook eggs in a saucepan of boiling water for 6 minutes (for soft boiled), drain and cool under running water. Peel and set aside.

step 3 Place the chicken, lettuce, onion and chives in a bowl and toss well to combine. Cut the eggs in half, place on the salad and spoon over the buttermilk dressing to serve. *Serves 4.*

try this...

MUSTARD DRESSING

Place 1 tablespoon Dijon mustard, 2 cloves crushed garlic, 2 tablespoons lemon juice and ¼ cup (60ml) olive oil in a bowl and whisk to combine. This dressing gives a punchier flavour. You could also add thinly sliced fennel and blanched asparagus to the basic salad recipe.

GARLIC DRESSING

Place 2 tablespoons white wine vinegar, 1 clove crushed garlic and ⅓ cup (80ml) olive oil in a bowl and whisk to combine. Perfect for a more pungent kick, this dressing also works well when more Mediterranean flavours are added to the salad, such as olives, goat's cheese and tomatoes.

cook's tip

For perfect soft boiled eggs, remember to add your eggs only once the water is boiling. It's a good idea to always use the freshest eggs you can find.

polenta

This humble dish is traditionally served as a side, but its nutty taste and delightfully creamy texture makes it the star of the show when paired with rich and robust flavours.

step 1

step 2

step 3

basic soft polenta

2 cups (500ml) chicken stock
1½ cups (375ml) milk
1 cup (170g) instant polenta
30g butter, chopped
¼ cup (20g) finely grated parmesan
sea salt and cracked black pepper

step 1 Place the stock and milk into a large saucepan over medium heat and bring to the boil.

step 2 Gradually whisk the polenta into the milk and stock mixture. (See *cook's tip*, below). Cook, stirring, for 2–3 minutes, or until thickened.

step 3 Remove from heat, add the butter, parmesan, salt and pepper, and stir to combine. *Serves 4.*

recipe notes...

CREATE A STIR
We've used instant polenta in our recipes. Instant polenta is made from precooked cornmeal; it's great for fast meals as it's ready in just a few minutes. But remember, polenta that isn't packaged as instant will take longer to cook and requires constant stirring for a longer period.

GET SET
After removing from the heat, the polenta will set and become firm on standing. If you're serving soft, creamy polenta it will need to be eaten straight away. If setting polenta, it's important to spread it out while it's still warm before allowing it to set.

cook's tip

It's very important to gradually add the polenta to the hot stock while continually whisking. This will prevent any lumps from forming and give the polenta a perfectly smooth texture.

herbed polenta chips

1 x quantity basic soft polenta (see recipe, page 28)
1 tablespoon chopped rosemary leaves
1 tablespoon oregano leaves
1 tablespoon thyme leaves
olive oil, for brushing
sea salt flakes, for sprinkling

Make the basic polenta, substituting the milk with 1½ cups (375ml) extra chicken stock⁺. Spoon into a lightly greased baking tray and spread to 1cm thick. Refrigerate for 30 minutes or until set.

Preheat oven to 220°C (425°F). Cut the polenta into 2cm x 10cm fingers, brush with oil and sprinkle with salt. Place on a lightly greased baking tray and bake for 20–25 minutes or until golden and crisp. Serve with mayonnaise or garlic aïoli, if desired. *Serves 4.*
+ *For this dish, you will need a total of 3½ cups (875ml) chicken stock*

grilled polenta with mushrooms and ricotta

1 x quantity basic soft polenta (see recipe, page 28)
4 field mushrooms
olive oil, for brushing
100g ricotta and store-bought pesto, to serve

Make the basic polenta, substituting the milk with 1½ cups (375ml) extra chicken stock⁺. Spoon into a lightly greased 20cm x 30cm tin lined with non-stick baking paper and smooth the top. Refrigerate for 30 minutes or until set.

Cut polenta into 6 pieces. Heat a char-grill pan or barbecue over high heat. Brush polenta and mushrooms with oil and char-grill or barbecue the mushrooms for 10 minutes. Remove from heat.

Char-grill or barbecue the polenta for 5–6 minutes each side or until golden. Serve polenta and mushrooms with the ricotta and drizzle with pesto. *Serves 4.*
+ *For this dish, you will need a total of 3½ cups (875ml) chicken stock.*

creamed corn polenta with crispy skin chicken

4 x 300g chicken supremes⁺, skin on
olive oil, for drizzling
5 sprigs sage
1 x quantity basic soft polenta (see recipe, page 28)
½ cup (130g) store-bought creamed corn
1 tablespoon chopped sage leaves, extra
steamed green beans, to serve

Preheat oven to 220°C (425°F). Place chicken on a baking tray, drizzle with olive oil and top with sage. Roast for 20–25 minutes or until golden and cooked through.

While the chicken is cooking, make the basic polenta, substituting the parmesan with ¼ cup (30g) cheddar. Add the corn and extra sage and stir to combine. Spoon onto plates, top with the chicken and sage and serve with green beans. *Serves 4.*
+ *A chicken supreme is a boneless cut of breast fillet with the wingtip still attached.*

one-pan chorizo, olive and feta polenta

1 x quantity basic soft polenta (see recipe, page 28)
2 tablespoons chopped basil leaves
1 chorizo, sliced
¼ cup (20g) pitted green olives, sliced
50g feta, crumbled
2 bocconcini, roughly torn
150g truss cherry tomatoes

Make the basic polenta. Add the basil and spoon into a 20cm frying pan with an ovenproof handle, top with the chorizo, olives, feta, bocconcini and tomatoes. Grill (broil) under a preheated hot grill (broiler) for 8 minutes or until top is golden and cheese is melted. *Serves 4.*

herbed polenta chips

creamed corn polenta
with crispy skin chicken

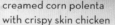

grilled polenta with
mushrooms and ricotta

one-pan chorizo, olive and feta polenta

gratin

This decadent dish with its layers of meltingly soft potato and creamy sauce is the perfect thing to give simple meals a little serve of indulgence.

step 1

step 2

potato gratin

½ cup (125ml) single (pouring) cream
½ cup (125ml) milk
¼ teaspoon ground nutmeg
20g butter, melted
600g desiree (waxy) potatoes
1 medium brown onion, peeled and finely sliced
2 cloves garlic, crushed
sea salt and cracked black pepper

step 1 Preheat oven to 180°C (350°F). Peel and thinly slice potatoes. Place the cream, milk and nutmeg in a saucepan over medium heat until just boiling. Remove from the heat.

step 2 Brush a 4 cup-capacity (1 litre) ovenproof dish with the butter and layer the potato, onion, garlic, salt and pepper in the dish, finishing with a layer of potato.

step 3 Pour over the warm cream mixture and bake for 45 minutes or until the potato is tender. *Serves 6.*

try this...

PARSNIP AND SWEET POTATO GRATIN
Place ¾ cup (45g) fresh breadcrumbs, 2 tablespoons melted butter, 2 teaspoons chopped rosemary, ⅓ cup (25g) finely grated parmesan and ¼ cup (40g) pine nuts in a bowl and mix until well combined. Set aside. Follow the basic gratin recipe, substituting 400g of the potato with 200g each peeled and finely sliced parsnips and sweet potato. Layer with the rosemary mixture.

cook's tip

Add a sprinkle of cheese between the layers of the basic recipe as you assemble the gratin to add flavour and help hold everything together. You can use your favourite cheese, from mild cheddar through to gruyère and parmesan or a sharp blue vein and goat's cheese. Finish with another layer of cheese to give added bite to the crunchy top layer.

filleting fish

You will need:
a cutting board
a sharp filleting knife
a small, sharp knife
fish bone tweezers

step 1 Using a sharp filleting knife, cut a diagonal line from the top of the head down past the pectoral fin. Extend the cut to the stomach to meet with the fishmonger's cut.

step 2 Place your hand firmly on the side of the fillet you're removing and, from the original cut at the top of the head, make a 1cm-deep cut along the length of the backbone to the tail.

step 3 Return to the original cut and slice the flesh away from the bones using a brushing motion. Allow the line of the bones to guide your knife and avoid sawing back and forth. Continue down the length of the fish to the tail. Protect your free hand with a folded tea towel while cutting. Cut through the tail. The fillet will still be connected at the belly cavity. Use the small knife to cut through the ribs and remove the fillet completely.

step 4 Turn the fish over to remove the second fillet and repeat step 1. This time the second cut is made from the tail along the length of backbone to meet the original cut at the head. Repeat steps 2 and 3.

step 5 Using fish bone tweezers, carefully remove the bones from both fillets.

caper and lemon butter snapper

1 tablespoon olive oil
1 x 1.3kg snapper, filleted and pin-boned
30g butter
2 tablespoons salted baby capers, rinsed and drained
1 tablespoon lemon juice
sea salt and cracked black pepper
baby spinach leaves and lemon wedges, to serve

Heat the oil in a non-stick frying pan over high heat. Add the fish, skin-side down first, and cook for 1–2 minutes each side or until cooked through. Remove fish from the pan and keep warm. Add the butter and capers and cook for 1 minute or until butter is golden. Add the lemon juice and remove from the heat. Drizzle the fish with the caper and lemon butter, sprinkle with salt and pepper and serve with the baby spinach leaves and lemon wedges. *Serves 2.*

step 1

step 4

baked risotto

With no stirring needed, a generous helping of creamy baked risotto is an effortless classic. Versatile and delicious, let this dish be a blank canvas for your culinary creativity.

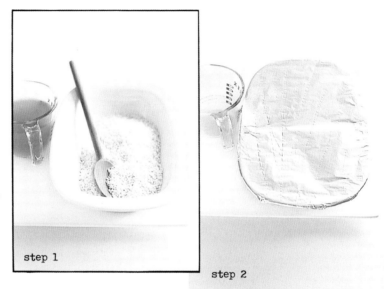

step 1

step 2

basic baked risotto

1½ cups (300g) arborio rice*
1.125 litres (4½ cups) chicken stock
1 cup (80g) finely grated parmesan
40g butter
sea salt and cracked black pepper

step 1 Preheat oven to 180°C (350°F). Place the rice and stock in a 10 cup-capacity (2.5 litre) baking dish and stir to combine.

step 2 Cover tightly with aluminium foil and bake for 40 minutes or until most of the stock is absorbed and the rice is al dente.

step 3 Stir through the parmesan, butter, salt and pepper and serve immediately. *Serves 4.*

tips + tricks

TO REHEAT
For best results, serve risotto immediately, but to reheat any leftover risotto, place in a saucepan on the stovetop, gradually add a little more stock and stir through gently until the risotto is heated through.

A GOLDEN IDEA
Risotto balls make great nibbles. Roll leftover risotto into balls, fill with blue cheese, mozzarella or parmesan, coat in breadcrumbs and deep-fry until golden.

CRISPY EXTRAS
Cook pancetta or prosciutto until crisp before crumbling over the top of your risotto for a rich and salty edge.

cook's tip
Resist the temptation to rinse the rice as you'll wash off the starch that gives it its deliciously creamy consistency. When adding the cheese, stir through gently, as vigorous stirring may result in a risotto without the perfect al dente bite.

pancetta, sweet potato and sage baked risotto

400g sweet potato (kumara), peeled and chopped
2 tablespoons olive oil
4 slices pancetta*
40g butter
¼ cup sage leaves
1½ cups (300g) arborio rice*
1.125 litres (4½ cups) chicken stock
1 cup (80g) finely grated parmesan
sea salt and cracked black pepper
melted butter, for drizzling

Preheat oven to 180°C (350°F). Place the sweet potato and 1 tablespoon oil on a baking tray and toss to coat. Roast for 25 minutes or until golden and tender. Set aside.

Heat a non-stick frying pan over medium heat. Add the remaining oil and pancetta and cook for 2–3 minutes or until crispy. Set aside. Melt the butter in a non-stick frying pan over medium heat. Add the sage and cook for 1–2 minutes or until crispy. Set aside.

Place the rice and stock in a 2.5 litre-capacity (10-cup) baking dish and stir to combine. Cover tightly with aluminium foil and cook for 40 minutes or until most of the stock is absorbed and the rice is al dente. Add the parmesan, salt and pepper, sweet potato and pancetta and stir to combine. Top with the sage, drizzle with the extra butter and serve immediately. *Serves 4.*

spinach, feta and pine nut baked risotto

1½ cups (300g) arborio rice*
1.125 litres (4½ cups) chicken stock
1 cup (80g) finely grated parmesan
40g butter
sea salt and cracked black pepper
50g baby spinach leaves
100g feta, crumbled
⅓ cup (50g) toasted pine nuts

Preheat oven to 180°C (350°F). Place the rice and stock in 2.5 litre-capacity (10-cup) baking dish and stir to combine. Cover tightly with aluminium foil and cook for 40 minutes or until most of the stock is absorbed and the rice is al dente. Add the parmesan, butter, salt and pepper, spinach, feta and pine nuts and stir until the butter is melted. Serve immediately. *Serves 4.*

mixed mushroom baked risotto

10g butter
2 tablespoons olive oil
2 cloves garlic, crushed
100g field mushrooms, sliced
100g Swiss brown mushrooms, sliced
100g button mushrooms, quartered
1½ cups (300g) arborio rice*
1.125 litres (4½ cups) chicken stock
1 cup (80g) finely grated parmesan
40g butter
sea salt and cracked black pepper

Heat a large non-stick frying pan over medium heat. Add the butter, oil, garlic and mushrooms and cook for 5 minutes or until the mushrooms are golden.

Preheat oven to 180°C (350°F). Place the rice, stock and mushroom mixture in a 2.5 litre-capacity (10-cup) baking dish and stir to combine. Cover tightly with aluminium foil and bake for 40 minutes or until most of the stock is absorbed and the rice is al dente. Add the parmesan, butter, salt and pepper and stir until the butter is melted. Serve immediately. *Serves 4.*

prawn, artichoke and lemon baked risotto

1½ cups (300g) arborio rice*
1.125 litres (4½ cups) chicken stock
16 medium green (raw) prawns (shrimp), peeled with tails intact
1 cup (80g) finely grated parmesan
40g butter
sea salt and cracked black pepper
2 teaspoons finely grated lemon rind
4 artichoke hearts, quartered
finely grated parmesan, extra, to serve

Preheat oven to 180°C (350°F). Place the rice and stock in a 2.5 litre-capacity (10-cup) baking dish and stir to combine. Cover tightly with aluminium foil and bake for 35 minutes. Add the prawns, cover and cook for a further 5 minutes or until most of the stock is absorbed and the rice is al dente. Add the parmesan, butter, salt and pepper, lemon rind and artichokes and stir until the butter is melted. Sprinkle with the extra parmesan and serve immediately. *Serves 4.*

gnocchi

Savour these soft and pillowy morsels with an array of delicious toppings. Prepared simply or baked in a rich tomato-based sauce, these cheat's dumplings are irresistible.

step 1

step 2

basic ricotta gnocchi

500g ricotta
½ cup (40g) finely grated parmesan
2 eggs, lightly beaten
1 cup (150g) plain (all-purpose) flour
sea salt and cracked black pepper

step 1 Place the ricotta, parmesan, eggs, flour, salt and pepper in a bowl and mix well to combine.

step 2 Turn the mixture out onto a lightly floured surface and roll into 4 x 15cm ropes. Cut the ropes into 2cm lengths and press lightly with the back of a fork.

step 3 Cook the gnocchi, in batches, in a large saucepan of salted boiling water for 2-3 minutes or until cooked through. Remove with a slotted spoon and place in bowls. Spoon over the oregano butter (see recipe, right) and toss to coat. *Serves 4.*

oregano butter

140g butter
1 cup oregano leaves
2 tablespoons white wine vinegar

Heat a small non-stick frying pan over medium heat. Add the butter and cook for 3-4 minutes or until the butter is golden brown. Add the oregano and vinegar and cook for a further 1 minute. Spoon the butter over the cooked gnocchi and toss gently to coat.

cook's tips

Gnocchi mixture can be prepared a day in advance. Roll out the dough and cut into pieces. Cover with plastic wrap and store in the fridge until you're ready to cook. Cook the gnocchi just before serving as this will keep them light and fluffy.

creamy mushroom gnocchi

prosciutto and spinach gnocchi

baked gnocchi

herb gnocchi with basil oil

creamy mushroom gnocchi

1 x quantity basic ricotta gnocchi (see recipe, page 38)
150g goat's cheese, crumbled
shaved parmesan, to serve
cracked black pepper, to serve
creamy mushroom sauce
1 tablespoon olive oil
1 small brown onion, chopped
300g button mushrooms, sliced
1¼ cups (310ml) single (pouring) cream
½ cup (125ml) chicken stock
1 tablespoon thyme leaves
sea salt and cracked black pepper

To make the creamy mushroom sauce, heat a medium non-stick frying pan over medium heat. Add the oil and onion and cook for 3 minutes or until the onion is softened. Stir in the mushrooms and cook for 5 minutes or until tender. Add the cream, stock, thyme, salt and pepper and simmer for 10 minutes or until the sauce is thickened. Set aside and keep warm.

Follow the basic gnocchi recipe, adding the goat's cheese to the mixture. Spoon the mushroom sauce over the cooked gnocchi and top with the parmesan and pepper to serve. *Serves 4.*

baked gnocchi

1 x quantity basic ricotta gnocchi (see recipe, page 38)
1 cup (100g) grated mozzarella
tomato sauce
1 tablespoon olive oil
3 garlic cloves, sliced
2 x 400g cans chopped tomatoes
1 cup (250ml) chicken stock
2 tablespoons brown sugar
400g can borlotti beans, drained
2 tablespoons chopped basil leaves
sea salt and cracked black pepper

To make the tomato sauce, heat a medium saucepan over medium heat. Add the oil and garlic and cook for 1–2 minutes. Add the tomatoes, stock and sugar and cook for 5–6 minutes. Add the beans, basil, salt and pepper and stir well to combine. Set aside.

Follow the basic gnocchi recipe. Place the cooked gnocchi in a 1 litre-capacity (4-cup) ovenproof dish. Spoon over the tomato sauce and top with the mozzarella. Cook under a preheated hot grill (broiler) for 3–4 minutes or until the cheese is melted and golden. *Serves 4.*

prosciutto and spinach gnocchi

1 x quantity basic ricotta gnocchi (see recipe, page 38)
1¼ teaspoons salted capers, rinsed, drained and chopped
2 anchovy fillets, chopped
50g butter
8 slices prosciutto, chopped
70g baby spinach leaves, chopped
1 tablespoon finely grated lemon rind
finely grated parmesan, to serve

Follow the basic gnocchi recipe, adding the capers and anchovies to the mixture. Cook the gnocchi and set aside.

Heat a large non-stick frying pan over medium heat. Add the butter and prosciutto and cook for 2–3 minutes or until crispy. Stir in the spinach and lemon rind, add the cooked gnocchi and toss to coat. Top with parmesan to serve. *Serves 4.*

herb gnocchi with basil oil

1 x quantity basic ricotta gnocchi (see recipe, page 38)
2 teaspoons shredded lemon zest
¼ cup chopped mint leaves
¼ cup chopped flat-leaf parsley leaves
¼ cup chopped basil leaves
sea salt and cracked black pepper
finely grated parmesan, to serve
basil oil
1 cup chopped basil leaves
½ cup (125ml) olive oil
2 tablespoons lemon juice
¼ cup (20g) grated parmesan
sea salt and cracked black pepper

To make the basil oil, place the basil, oil, lemon juice, parmesan, salt and pepper in the bowl of a food processor and process until finely chopped. Set aside.

Follow the basic gnocchi recipe, adding the lemon zest, mint, parsley, basil, salt and pepper to the mixture. Spoon the basil oil over the cooked gnocchi and toss to coat. Top with the parmesan to serve. *Serves 4.*

essentials

tomato sauce

cooked rice

couscous

roasted garlic

onion relish

curry paste

gravy

aïoli

salsa verde

terrine

chicken liver pâté

blini

carpaccio

rice paper rolls

frittata

flatbread

tomato sauce

Easy to cook and full of vibrant flavour, this fresh staple is ideal for quick pasta sauces or as a base for pizza. It's so good you'll want to start bottling your own.

step 1

step 2

fresh tomato sauce

1kg vine-ripened Roma tomatoes
5 cloves garlic, unpeeled
2 tablespoons extra-virgin olive oil
1 teaspoon red wine vinegar
1 teaspoon caster (superfine) sugar
sea salt and cracked black pepper
1 cup basil leaves

step 1 Preheat oven to 200°C (400°F). Using a small, sharp knife, cut a shallow 2cm cross in the base of each tomato. Place the tomatoes and garlic in a baking dish lined with non-stick baking paper and roast for 15–20 minutes or until the tomatoes are tender and their skins start to peel away. Allow to cool slightly.

step 2 Peel the tomatoes and garlic and roughly chop. Place in a bowl with the oil, vinegar, sugar, salt, pepper and basil and stir to combine. *Makes 2¾ cups (680ml).*

try this...

AS A BASE
This chunky sauce makes a delicious base for pizza and, with a few added ingredients, also makes fantastic pasta sauce or a base for a meat braise such as osso bucco. For a finer, smoother textured sauce, place the finished sauce in a food processor and process until smooth.

IN A SEAFOOD PASTA
Bring the tomato sauce to the boil, add peeled green (raw) prawns (shrimp) and cook for 2–3 minutes or until the prawns are cooked through. Serve with cooked fettucine or penne.

recipe notes

Keep your fresh tomato sauce in an airtight container in the fridge for up to 4 days. The sauce can be re-heated over low heat before using for a quick pasta sauce or a spread for pizza.

rice

1½ cups (300g) long grain or jasmine rice
2½ cups (625ml) water

Place the rice and cold water in a large saucepan with a tight-fitting lid over medium heat. Cook for 10–12 minutes, until 'tunnels' form in the rice and the water is almost completely absorbed. Remove the saucepan from the heat and set aside for 5–10 minutes with the lid on. Fluff up with a fork to separate the grains and serve. *Serves 4.*
Tip: To freeze, spread the cooked rice out on a tray lined with baking paper, fluff with a fork to separate the grains and cool before freezing in plastic airtight containers. To defrost, place in the refrigerator and use for a fast dinner or an easy side.

couscous

1½ cups (300g) instant couscous
1½ cups (375ml) hot water or chicken stock
30g butter
sea salt and cracked black pepper

Place the couscous and water or stock in a bowl and cover with plastic wrap or a tight-fitting lid. Set aside for 5 minutes or until the liquid is absorbed. Add the butter, salt and pepper and use a fork to fluff the couscous and separate the grains. *Serves 4.*
Tip: Using chicken stock will give your couscous more flavour. You can also add your favourite spices, fresh or dried herbs, currants or pine nuts with the butter. Use the cooked couscous to make salads or serve as a side to stews or grilled meats.

onion relish

⅓ cup (80ml) olive oil
2kg brown onions, sliced
1 cup (175g) brown sugar
1 cup (250ml) red wine vinegar
sea salt and cracked black pepper

Preheat a large, deep saucepan over medium–high heat. Add the oil and onion, cover and cook, stirring occasionally, for 40 minutes or until the onion is golden and caramelised. Add the sugar, vinegar, salt and pepper and stir until the sugar is dissolved. Cook for a further 10 minutes or until thick and syrupy. Pour the mixture into sterilised glass jars. *Makes 1.25 litres.*
Tip: Your relish will keep unopened for one month in a cool, dark place. Once opened, it will keep in the refrigerator for up to three months. Bring to room temperature before using.

roasted garlic

3 heads garlic
1 tablespoon olive oil
char-grilled bread, to serve

Preheat oven to 180°C (350°F). Cut the tops off the garlic heads so the cloves are just showing. Drizzle with olive oil and wrap in aluminium foil. Place on a baking tray and roast for 45 minutes or until soft. Set aside to cool slightly before peeling off the skins+.
Place the cloves in a bowl and mash with the back of a fork.
Spread on char-grilled bread to serve.
+ *The garlic will be so soft and jammy that you'll be able to press the flesh out by gently squeezing the cloves. You can also use the roasted garlic in sauces or serve with roasted meats or vegies.*

curry paste

This staple of the Asian kitchen is not only a great base for a rich curry, it's perfect for marinating barbecued meats. It also freezes well for future use.

step 1   step 3

green curry paste

½ teaspoon ground cumin
½ teaspoon ground coriander (cilantro)
¼ teaspoon ground turmeric*
1 teaspoon shrimp paste*
1 onion or 5 green onions (scallions), chopped
2 stalks lemongrass*, white part only, sliced
4 kaffir lime leaves*, shredded
2 teaspoons grated ginger
4 long green chillies (2 seeded), chopped
2 tablespoons chopped coriander (cilantro) root
¾ cup coriander (cilantro) leaves
2 teaspoons brown sugar
sea salt and cracked black pepper
2 tablespoons peanut oil

step 1 Place the cumin, ground coriander, turmeric and shrimp paste in a small non-stick frying pan over medium heat. Cook, stirring to break up the shrimp paste, for 2–3 minutes or until aromatic.

step 2 Place the spice mixture in a food processor with the onion, lemongrass, kaffir lime leaves, ginger, chillies, coriander root and leaves, sugar, salt and pepper and process until combined.

step 3 With the motor running, gradually add the oil in a thin stream until a smooth paste forms. *Makes approx. 1 cup (250ml).*

try this...

THAI CHICKEN CURRY
Cook 3 tablespoons of the curry paste in 1 tablespoon oil over medium-high heat for 1 minute or until fragrant. Add 500g chopped chicken thigh fillets and cook until browned. Add 1 cup (250ml) coconut cream and ¾ cup (180ml) chicken stock and simmer, covered, for 20 minutes. Add 1 bunch chopped snake beans and cook until tender. Serve with steamed rice and coriander (cilantro) leaves. *Serves 4.*

AS A MARINADE
You can use your aromatic curry paste for more than traditional curries. Try using it as a marinade for meats, such as lamb, fish or beef before char-grilling or barbecuing.

some for later
Store your curry paste in a clean, dry airtight container in the fridge for up to 2 months. Divide any unused paste into portions and freeze for up to 3 months.

gravy

What would roasted meats be without a delicious gravy? Master the basic and then add your favourite flavours such as mustard, red wine and more.

step 1   step 2

basic gravy

1 tablespoon pan juices or vegetable oil
2 tablespoons plain (all-purpose) flour
2 cups (500ml) chicken stock
1 teaspoon tomato paste
1 teaspoon caster (superfine) sugar
2 bay leaves
6 black peppercorns

step 1 Heat the pan juices or oil in a deep frying pan over low heat. Add the flour and cook, stirring occasionally, for 5-7 minutes or until golden and sandy in texture.

step 2 Gradually whisk in the stock. Add the tomato paste, sugar, bay leaves and peppercorns, increase the heat to medium and cook for a further 5 minutes or until thickened. Serve with chicken, turkey or pork. *Makes 2 cups (500ml).*

try this...
RED WINE GRAVY
Gradually whisk in ½ cup (125ml) red wine with the other ingredients at step 2. Serve with steak or sausages and mashed potato. The quality of wine affects the flavour of the gravy, so use a nice drop that you would be happy to drink.

MUSTARD AND BRANDY GRAVY
Carefully whisk in ½ cup (125ml) brandy, and 1 tablespoon seeded mustard at step 2. Try this mustard-flavoured gravy with roasted chicken, turkey or pork.

cook's tips
Always use a whisk when adding liquids to the flour and oil to avoid a lumpy gravy. If you do end up with flour lumps, pass the gravy through a fine sieve and discard the solids.

aïoli

1 egg
1 tablespoon lemon juice
3 cloves garlic, crushed
1 cup (250ml) vegetable oil
sea salt flakes

Place the egg, lemon juice and garlic in a food processor or blender and process until well combined. With the motor running, pour the oil in, slowly, in a thin stream and process until the mixture is thick and creamy. Add salt and combine. *Makes 1¼ cups (310ml).*
Tip: You can serve this as a tasty dipping sauce for barbecued prawns, grilled meats and fish or as a spread on a sandwich.

salsa verde

1 cup flat-leaf parsley leaves
1 tablespoon salted capers, rinsed and drained
1 small clove garlic, chopped
1 teaspoon Dijon mustard
2 anchovy fillets (optional)
1 tablespoon lemon juice
1 tablespoon olive oil

Place the parsley, capers, garlic, mustard and anchovies, if using, in the bowl of a food processor and process until roughly chopped. With the motor running, gradually add the lemon juice and oil and process until well combined. *Makes ½ cup (125ml).*
Tip: Use this basic green sauce as an accompaniment to roasted lamb, grilled steak or chicken. You can also use it as a marinade.

terrine

This rustic French classic is ideal for entertaining,
makes an impressive alternative to pâté and can be cooked
with a variety of meats and flavours. Bon appétit!

step 1

step 2

step 3

basic country-style terrine

800g coarse veal mince
800g coarse pork mince
3 rashers bacon, rind removed and finely chopped
3 cloves garlic, crushed
2 tablespoons lemon thyme leaves
1 tablespoon sea salt flakes
2 teaspoons cracked black pepper
½ cup (125ml) brandy
3 eggs
16–20 slices prosciutto

step 1 Preheat oven to 180°C (350°F). Place the minces, bacon, garlic, lemon thyme, salt, pepper, brandy and eggs in a large bowl and mix well to combine.

step 2 Line a lightly greased 32cm x 8cm x 8cm loaf tin with prosciutto, overlapping the pieces slightly. Press the mince mixture into the tin and fold over the prosciutto to enclose. Cover with aluminium foil, place in a deep baking dish and pour in enough hot water to come halfway up the sides of the tin. Cook for 1½ hours or until firm. Remove the tin from the water.

step 3 Cut a piece of cardboard to fit over the terrine, weigh down with a heavy object (such as canned vegetables) and refrigerate overnight. Remove the terrine from the tin and slice to serve. *Serves 10–12.*

try this...
ACCOMPANIMENTS
You can serve terrine with dill pickles (gherkins) or cornichons, pickled onions and chutneys, mustard fruits or relishes. For a casual lunch or snack, serve with toasted baguettes, crisp flatbread, or loaves of country-style bread.

recipe notes
A properly cooked terrine should be slightly pink in colour. Run a blunt knife around the outside of the terrine so it slides out of the tin more easily. Cover with plastic wrap and store your terrine in the refrigerator for up to 5 days.

leek and pink peppercorn terrine

400g coarse veal mince
400g coarse pork mince
1 rasher bacon, rind removed, finely chopped
1 clove garlic, crushed
1 tablespoon thyme leaves
1 tablespoon whole pink peppercorns, finely crushed
2 teaspoons sea salt flakes
1 teaspoon cracked black pepper
⅓ cup (80ml) sweet sherry
2 eggs
3 leeks, halved lengthwise, blanched and separated

Preheat oven to 180°C (350°F). Place the veal and pork mince, bacon, garlic, thyme, peppercorns, salt, pepper, sherry and eggs in a large bowl and mix well to combine. Line 8 x ¾ cup-capacity (180ml) lightly greased loaf tins with the leek. Follow steps 2 and 3 of the basic recipe and adjust the cooking time to 30 minutes. Refrigerate for 4 hours or until cold. Remove the terrines from the tins to serve. *Makes 8.*

caramelised apple and pork terrines

25g butter
⅓ cup (60g) brown sugar
3 teaspoons water
400g coarse chicken mince
400g coarse pork mince
1 rasher bacon, rind removed, finely chopped
1 clove garlic, crushed
2 teaspoons sea salt flakes
1 teaspoon cracked black pepper
¼ cup (60ml) Marsala*
2 eggs
1 tablespoon sage leaves
2 x 140g small red apples, sliced

Preheat oven to 180°C (350°F). Place the butter, sugar and water in a small saucepan over medium heat and stir until the butter is melted. Bring to the boil and cook for 1-2 minutes or until thickened slightly. Set aside.
   Place the chicken, pork, bacon, garlic, salt, pepper, Marsala and eggs in a large bowl and mix well to combine. Line 6 x 1 cup-capacity (250ml) lightly greased muffin tins with thin strips of non-stick baking paper. Divide the caramel mixture between the tins, top with sage and apple slices and press the mince mixture into the tin. Follow steps 2 and 3 of the basic recipe and adjust cooking time to 45 minutes. Refrigerate for 4 hours or until cold. Use the strips of baking paper to remove the terrines from the tins to serve. *Makes 6.*

chicken and pistachio terrine

800g coarse chicken mince
800g coarse pork mince
3 rashers bacon, rind removed and finely chopped
3 cloves garlic, crushed
2 tablespoons chopped tarragon leaves
1½ cups (195g) dried cranberries
½ cup (70g) shelled unsalted pistachios
1 tablespoon sea salt flakes
2 teaspoons cracked black pepper
½ cup (125ml) port
3 eggs

Preheat oven to 180°C (350°F). Place the chicken and pork mince, bacon, garlic, tarragon, cranberries, pistachios, salt, pepper, port and eggs in a large bowl and mix well to combine. Follow steps 2 and 3 of the basic recipe, cooking for 1½ hours. Refrigerate overnight. Remove the terrine from the dish and slice to serve. *Serves 10-12.*

veal and duck terrine

4 x 225g duck breast fillets, skin off
olive oil, for brushing
sea salt and cracked black pepper
1.2kg coarse veal mince
2 rashers bacon, rind removed and finely chopped
3 cloves garlic, crushed
2 tablespoons marjoram leaves
1 tablespoon sea salt flakes
2 teaspoons cracked black pepper
½ cup (125ml) brandy
3 eggs
10-12 rashers bacon, extra, rind removed

Preheat oven to 180°C (350°F). Heat a large non-stick frying pan over high heat. Brush the duck with oil, sprinkle with salt and pepper and cook for 1 minute each side. Set aside.
   Place the veal mince, bacon, garlic, marjoram, salt, pepper, brandy and eggs in a large bowl and mix well to combine. Line a lightly greased 8 cup-capacity (2 litre) loaf tin with bacon, overlapping the pieces slightly. Press half the mince mixture into the tin and top with the duck. Top with the remaining mince mixture, fold over the bacon to enclose and cover with aluminium foil. Place in a deep baking dish and pour in enough hot water to come halfway up the sides of the tin. Cook for 1½ hours or until firm. Remove from the water, weigh down with a heavy object and refrigerate overnight. Remove the terrine from the tin and slice to serve. *Serves 10-12.*

leek and pink peppercorn terrine

chicken and pistachio terrine

caramelised apple and pork terrines

veal and duck terrine

chicken liver pâté

20g butter
2 cloves garlic, crushed
1 small brown onion, chopped
300g chicken livers, trimmed (see *recipe notes*, below)
¼ cup (60ml) brandy
125g cold butter, extra, chopped
¼ cup (60ml) double (thick) cream
sea salt and cracked black pepper
80g clarified butter (see below)
toasted rye bread and cornichons, to serve

step 1 Place the butter, garlic and onion in a large non-stick frying pan over medium heat and cook for 2–3 minutes or until softened. Add the livers and cook for 1 minute. Add the brandy and cook for a further 1 minute.

step 2 Place the liver mixture, extra cold butter, cream, salt and pepper in the bowl of a food processor and process until smooth.

step 3 Press the mixture through a fine sieve and spoon into 2 x 1 cup-capacity (250ml) round dishes

step 4 Pour over the clarified butter and refrigerate for 2 hours or until set. Serve with rye bread and cornichons. *Serves 4.*

clarified butter

To make clarified butter, melt the butter gently over a very low heat without stirring. Remove from the heat and allow to stand. As the butter cools, the milk solids will settle to the bottom, leaving a clear golden liquid. Without disturbing the milk solids, spoon off the clear clarified butter and spoon over the pâté.

step 2   step 3

recipe notes
Chicken liver comes in 2 'lobes'. Trim away any white connective tissue and bloodlines to ensure your pâté doesn't taste bitter.

blini

These fluffy buckwheat pancakes are great hand-held party starters and are a blank canvas for your favourite toppings from cream cheese to salmon.

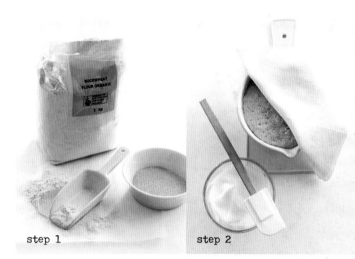

step 1

step 2

basic blini

⅔ cup (100g) plain (all-purpose) flour, sifted
¼ cup (35g) buckwheat flour*, sifted
½ teaspoon table salt
1 teaspoon active dry yeast*
½ cup (125ml) milk
⅓ cup (80g) sour cream
1 egg, separated

step 1 Place both the flours, salt and yeast in a bowl and stir to combine. Place the milk and sour cream in a saucepan over low heat and cook, stirring, for 2 minutes or until lukewarm. Add the egg yolk and whisk to combine. Gradually add the milk mixture to the flour mixture, stirring until smooth.

step 2 Cover with a clean, damp cloth and set aside in a warm place for 30 minutes or until bubbles appear on the surface.

step 3 Whisk the eggwhite until soft peaks form, add to the mixture and stir well to combine.

step 4 Heat a lightly greased, large non-stick frying pan over medium heat. Cook teaspoonfuls of the mixture for 1–2 minutes or until bubbles appear on the surface. Flip and cook for 1–2 minutes or until golden. Allow to cool. *Makes 30.*

try this…

SMOKED TROUT, CAPER AND DILL BLINI
For a chic party starter, top blini with a dollop of sour cream, rinsed salted capers, dill sprigs and smoked trout.

RICOTTA BLINI WITH PESTO AND FETA
Fold ½ cup (100g) fresh ricotta through the blini mixture. Cook and top with store-bought pesto, crumbled feta and watercress sprigs to serve.

EGG AND SALMON BRUNCH BLINI
For a delicious breakfast option, top cooked blinis with scrambled eggs, salmon roe, chervil, sea salt and cracked pepper.

carpaccio

This dish of paper-thin slices of raw beef or fish is a lovely light start to a meal. The technique is easy and best of all, there's little or no cooking involved.

step 1

step 2

beef carpaccio

250g beef eye fillet, trimmed
sea salt and cracked black pepper
1 tablespoon olive oil
¼ cup (50g) salted capers,
rinsed and drained
4 pickled onions, thinly sliced
½ cup chopped flat-leaf parsley leaves
extra-virgin olive oil, for drizzling
finely grated parmesan, to serve

step 1 Sprinkle the beef with salt and pepper, wrap in plastic wrap and place in the freezer for 1 hour or until just frozen. Heat the oil in a non-stick frying pan over high heat. Add the capers and cook for 3–4 minutes or until crispy. Drain on absorbent paper and allow to cool.

step 2 Unwrap the beef and use a very sharp knife to thinly slice. Arrange on plates and top with the capers, onion and parsley, drizzle with the oil and sprinkle with parmesan to serve. *Serves 4.*

tips + tricks

FREEZING
Freezing the beef before cooking makes it easier to cut paper-thin slices. The beef thaws very quickly once sliced.

EXTRA FLAVOUR
The little or no cooking involved in making carpaccio lends itself to being served with condiments that add flavour and texture to the dish. Try thinly sliced radish and fennel or crispy capers.

FOR A TOUCH OF GLAMOUR
Arrange slices of scallop, scampi or lobster carpaccio on a heatproof plate, drizzle with olive oil and grill (broil) under a preheated hot grill (broiler) for 15 seconds.

kitchen notes

Try serving your carpaccio with sauces that have a little bite, such as mustard and horseradish cream for beef or an infused olive oil for fish. Top with herbs to complete the dish.

seared beef fillet with horseradish cream

300g beef eye fillet
2 tablespoons cracked black pepper
1 tablespoon olive oil
1 cup watercress sprigs
½ cup store-bought baby beetroots, sliced
horseradish cream
1 cup (240g) crème fraîche*
1½ tablespoons store-bought grated horseradish
2 tablespoons lemon juice

To make the horseradish cream, combine the crème fraîche, horseradish and lemon juice in a bowl. Set aside.

Roll the beef in the pepper. Heat the oil in a non-stick frying pan over high heat. Cook the beef for 1–2 minutes on each side or until browned. Cover with aluminium foil and set aside for 5 minutes to rest. Use a very sharp knife to thinly slice the beef. Arrange on plates with the watercress and beetroot and serve with the horseradish cream. *Serves 4.*

kingfish, chilli and fennel carpaccio

1 tablespoon sea salt flakes
1 teaspoon fennel seeds, crushed
½ teaspoon dried chilli flakes
250g kingfish fillet, trimmed and pin-boned
1 bulb baby fennel, thinly sliced and fronds reserved for garnish
⅓ cup (80ml) lemon-flavoured extra-virgin olive oil
lemon wedges, to serve

Combine the salt, fennel seeds and chilli flakes in a bowl and set aside. Use a very sharp knife to thinly slice the kingfish. Arrange on 4 serving plates with the fennel, sprinkle with the salt mixture and garnish with reserved fennel fronds. Drizzle with the oil and serve with lemon wedges. *Serves 4.*
Tip: It's important to use the best sashimi-grade fish you can lay your hands on. Use a large, thin-bladed, bendable knife to slice the fish. Your fishmonger can pin-bone the fish for you.

salmon with miso dressing

30g ginger, peeled and thinly sliced
2 eschalots* (French shallots), peeled and thinly sliced
1 long red chilli, seeds removed and thinly sliced
¼ cup (35g) cornflour (cornstarch)
2 tablespoons vegetable oil
250g salmon fillet, trimmed and pin-boned
coriander (cilantro) leaves, to garnish
miso dressing
2 teaspoons white miso paste*
½ cup (125ml) water
1 teaspoon soy sauce

To make the miso dressing, place the miso, water and soy sauce in a small saucepan over low heat and stir to combine. Cook for 1–2 minutes or until warmed through. Set aside and allow to cool.

Place the ginger, eschalot, chilli and cornflour in a bowl and toss to coat, shaking off excess. Heat the oil in a small non-stick frying pan over high heat. Add the ginger mixture and cook for 2–3 minutes or until crispy. Drain on absorbent paper and set aside. Use a very sharp knife to thinly slice the salmon. Arrange on plates, top with the crispy ginger mixture and coriander and spoon over the miso dressing to serve. *Serves 4.*

tuna with sesame and teriyaki dressing

250g tuna fillet, trimmed
1 cup (150g) sesame seeds
1 tablespoon vegetable oil
pickled ginger*, to serve
teriyaki dressing
½ cup (125ml) dry white wine
½ cup (125ml) soy sauce
2 tablespoons caster (superfine) sugar
1 tablespoon Chinese black vinegar*
½ teaspoon sesame oil

To make the teriyaki dressing, place the wine, soy sauce, sugar, vinegar, and sesame oil in a small saucepan over high heat and cook, stirring to dissolve the sugar, for 2–3 minutes or until thickened slightly. Set aside and allow to cool.

Roll the piece of tuna in the sesame seeds until well coated. Heat the oil in a non-stick frying pan over high heat. Add the tuna and cook for 30 seconds on each side. Use a very sharp knife to thinly slice the tuna. Arrange on plates and serve with the teriyaki dressing and pickled ginger. *Serves 4.*

rice paper rolls

These Vietnamese classics are the ultimate finger food and can be filled with all manner of treats, from fresh vegies and noodles to tasty duck, beef or chicken.

step 1

step 2

step 2

basic vegetable rolls

50g dried rice vermicelli noodles*
8 x 16cm diameter rice paper rounds*
¼ cup mint leaves
¼ cup coriander (cilantro) leaves
1 green onion (scallion), trimmed and thinly sliced
1 carrot (100g), peeled and thinly sliced
1 Lebanese cucumber, thinly sliced
50g snow peas (mange tout), blanched and thinly sliced
1 long red chilli, seeds removed and thinly sliced (optional)

step 1 Place the noodles in a bowl and cover with boiling water. Allow to stand for 6–8 minutes or until tender. Drain and return to the bowl. Set aside.

step 2 Soften a rice paper round in warm water for 30 seconds. Place on a dry, clean cloth. Top with mint, coriander, green onion, carrot, cucumber, snow peas, chilli and noodles. Fold over one end and then roll to enclose filling. Repeat with remaining ingredients, being careful not to over-fill the rolls. Serve with the vinegar and soy dipping sauce (see recipes, right). *Makes 8.*

dipping sauces

LIME AND CHILLI

Combine ⅓ cup (80ml) lime juice, 2 small sliced red chillies, ¼ cup (60ml) fish sauce and 2 teaspoons caster (superfine) sugar in a bowl. Serve with chicken, beef or vegetable rice paper rolls. *Makes ½ cup (125ml).*

VINEGAR AND SOY

Combine ⅓ cup (80ml) rice wine vinegar, 2 tablespoons soy sauce and 1 small sliced red chilli in a bowl. Serve with beef, chicken, duck or vegetable rice paper rolls. *Makes ½ cup (125ml).*

cook's tip

Be sure to assemble the rolls just before you serve and keep them covered with a clean, damp tea towel once they have been made. This will prevent them from drying out and splitting.

ginger pork parcels

five-spice duck rolls

coconut and chilli chicken rolls

basil and lime beef rolls

ginger pork parcels

⅓ cup (80ml) hoisin sauce*
2 teaspoons finely grated ginger
2 tablespoons soy sauce
400g pork fillet, trimmed
2 teaspoons vegetable oil
8 x 22cm diameter rice paper rounds*
½ cup Vietnamese mint leaves*
100g snow peas (mange tout), trimmed, blanched and finely sliced

Preheat oven to 180°C (350°F). Combine the hoisin, ginger and soy in a small bowl. Place half the mixture in a separate bowl with the pork and toss to coat. Heat a non-stick frying pan over medium heat, add the oil and pork and cook for 2 minutes each side. Transfer to the oven and cook for a further 10–12 minutes or to your liking. Allow to cool for 5 minutes before slicing.

Soften a rice paper round in warm water for 30 seconds. Place on a dry, clean cloth. Top with mint, pork and snow peas and spoon over some of the remaining hoisin mixture. Fold over one end and fold over each side to form an open-ended parcel. Repeat with remaining ingredients. *Makes 8.*

coconut and chilli chicken rolls

1 x 400g can coconut milk
2 tablespoons fish sauce
2 tablespoons lime juice
1 small red chilli, chopped
2 x 200g chicken breast fillets, trimmed
8 x 22cm diameter rice paper rounds*
1 cup Vietnamese mint leaves*
1 green onion (scallion), trimmed and thinly sliced
2 cups (160g) bean sprouts
2 small red chillies, extra, seeds removed and thinly sliced

Combine the coconut milk, fish sauce, lime juice and chilli in a deep frying pan over medium heat. Bring to the boil, add the chicken and cover with a tight-fitting lid. Reduce the heat to low and cook for 8–10 minutes or until the chicken is cooked through. Remove from the pan, reserving the coconut sauce. Allow the chicken to cool slightly and then shred. Set aside.

Soften a rice paper round in warm water for 30 seconds. Place on a dry, clean cloth. Top with mint, green onion, shredded chicken, bean sprouts and chilli. Fold over each end and roll to enclose filling. Repeat with remaining ingredients. Slice rice paper rolls in half and serve with the reserved coconut sauce. *Makes 8.*

five-spice duck rolls

2 x 230g duck breast fillets, skin on, trimmed
1 teaspoon Chinese five-spice powder*
sea salt and cracked black pepper
¼ cup (60ml) plum sauce
½ teaspoon rice wine vinegar*
50g dried rice vermicelli noodles*
8 x 16cm diameter rice paper rounds*
½ cup coriander (cilantro) leaves
8 garlic chives*, cut into thirds, plus extra, for tying
4 Chinese cabbage (wombok) leaves*, blanched and halved

Preheat oven to 180°C (350°F). Sprinkle duck skin with the five-spice, salt and pepper. Heat a medium non-stick frying pan over high heat. Add the duck, skin-side down, and cook for 3–4 minutes each side or until browned. Transfer to the oven and cook for a further 5–8 minutes or until cooked through. Cool for 5 minutes before slicing.

Combine the plum sauce and vinegar in a small bowl and set aside. Place the noodles in a bowl and cover with boiling water. Allow to stand for 6–8 minutes or until soft. Drain and set aside.

Soften a rice paper round in warm water for 30 seconds. Place on a dry, clean cloth. Top with coriander, chives, cabbage, duck and noodles and spoon over some of the plum sauce mixture. Fold over each end and roll to enclose filling. Repeat with remaining ingredients. Tie each roll with a garlic chive to serve. *Makes 8.*

basil and lime beef rolls

⅓ cup (80ml) oyster sauce
2 tablespoons lime juice
300g beef fillet
2 teaspoons vegetable oil
4 x 22cm diameter rice paper rounds*
1 cup Thai basil leaves*
200g enoki mushrooms*
1 Lebanese cucumber, halved and sliced

Preheat oven to 180°C (350°F). Combine the oyster sauce and lime juice in a bowl. Place half of the mixture in a separate bowl with the beef and toss to coat. Heat a medium non-stick frying pan over high heat. Add the oil and beef and cook for 2 minutes each side. Transfer to the oven and cook for a further 5 minutes for medium-rare or until cooked to your liking. Allow to cool for 5 minutes before slicing.

Soften a rice paper round in warm water for 30 seconds. Place on a dry, clean cloth. Halve the rice paper and top each half with basil, beef, mushrooms and cucumber and spoon over remaining oyster sauce mixture. Fold over the rounded end of rice paper half and roll to enclose filling. Repeat with remaining ingredients. Serve with lime and chilli dipping sauce (see recipe, page 60). *Makes 8.*

frittata

Not just a breakfast treat, frittata also makes a great
light lunch served with a simple salad, or once cooled
turns into a portable picnic or lunchbox snack.

three cheese frittata

6 eggs
1 cup (250ml) single (pouring) cream
⅓ cup (25g) finely grated parmesan
sea salt and cracked black pepper
20g butter
2 teaspoons olive oil
400g ricotta
1 cup (120g) grated cheddar

step 1

step 2

step 1 Place the eggs, cream, parmesan,
salt and pepper in a bowl and whisk to
combine. Heat a 22cm ovenproof non-stick
frying pan over low heat. Add the butter and
oil and swirl around the pan to coat. Add the
egg mixture and cook for 5 minutes or until
the edges just start to set.

step 2 Top with the ricotta and cheddar
and cook for 15 minutes or until the egg
is almost set. Place under a preheated hot
grill (broiler) for 5 minutes or until the egg
is set and the top is golden. *Serves 4.*

try this...

CHEESE
For a more grown-up and intense flavour,
crumble a Stilton or blue brie through the
mixture. You can also use goat's curd or
cheese for a milder flavour.

ADDITIONS
For a more generous frittata, you can add
a host of leftovers or try adding roasted
vegetables, barbecued chicken, meat, fish,
canned tuna, smoked salmon, ham, salami,
chorizo or barbecued sausages.

cook's tip
Make sure you use a frying pan with an ovenproof handle before
baking or grilling your frittata in the oven, so the handle
doesn't melt or catch on fire.

roasted pumpkin and feta frittata

500g butternut pumpkin, peeled and sliced
2 tablespoons olive oil
sea salt and cracked black pepper
6 eggs
1 cup (250ml) single (pouring) cream
⅓ cup (25g) grated parmesan
sea salt and cracked black pepper, extra
2 x 200g chicken breast fillets, cooked and shredded
200g feta, crumbled

Preheat oven to 180°C (350°F). Place the pumpkin, oil, salt and pepper in a bowl and toss to coat. Place on 2 baking trays and roast for 15 minutes or until golden. Place the eggs, cream, parmesan, salt and pepper in a bowl and whisk to combine. Layer the pumpkin, chicken and feta in 12 x ½ cup-capacity (125ml) lightly greased muffin tins and pour over the egg mixture. Bake for 15–20 minutes or until the egg is set and the top is golden. *Makes 12.*

asparagus, potato and goat's cheese frittata

800g sebago (starchy) potatoes, peeled and cut into wedges
2 tablespoons olive oil
16 spears asparagus, trimmed and chopped
6 eggs
1 cup (250ml) single (pouring) cream
⅓ cup (25g) finely grated parmesan
sea salt and cracked black pepper
110g goat's cheese, crumbled

Preheat oven to 180°C (350°F). Place the potatoes and oil in a 1.5 litre (6 cup) capacity ceramic baking dish and toss to coat. Cook for 45 minutes or until golden. Top with the asparagus. Place the eggs, cream, parmesan, salt and pepper in a bowl and whisk to combine. Pour the egg mixture over the potatoes and asparagus and top with the goat's cheese. Cook for 15–20 minutes or until the egg is set and the top is golden. *Serves 4.*

pea, pancetta, leek and onion frittata

20g butter
2 teaspoons olive oil
1 brown onion, sliced
1 leek, sliced
6 eggs
1 cup (250ml) single (pouring) cream
⅓ cup (25g) finely grated parmesan
sea salt and cracked black pepper
200g ricotta
1 cup (120g) frozen peas, defrosted
5 slices pancetta*, roughly chopped

Heat a 22cm ovenproof non-stick frying pan over medium heat. Add the butter and oil and swirl around the pan to coat. Add the onion and leek and cook, stirring, for 5 minutes or until soft. Place the eggs, cream, parmesan, salt and pepper in a bowl and whisk to combine. Reduce the heat to low, pour over the egg mixture and cook for 5 minutes or until the edges just start to set. Top with the ricotta, peas and pancetta and cook for 15 minutes or until the egg is almost set. Place under a preheated hot grill (broiler) for 5 minutes or until the egg is set and the top is golden. *Serves 4.*

grated zucchini frittata

6 eggs
1 cup (250ml) single (pouring) cream
⅓ cup (25g) finely grated parmesan, plus extra, to serve
sea salt and cracked black pepper
20g butter
2 teaspoons olive oil
3 zucchinis (courgettes), grated

Place the eggs, cream, parmesan, salt and pepper in a bowl and whisk to combine. Heat a 22cm ovenproof non-stick frying pan over low heat. Add the butter and oil and swirl around the pan to coat. Add the egg mixture and cook for 5 minutes or until the edges just start to set. Top with the zucchini and cook for 15 minutes or until the egg is almost set. Place under a preheated hot grill (broiler) for 5 minutes or until the egg is set and the top is golden. Sprinkle with extra parmesan to serve. *Serves 4.*

roasted pumpkin and feta frittata

pea, pancetta, leek and onion frittata

asparagus, potato and goat's cheese frittata

grated zucchini frittata

flatbread

The crisp crust and fluffy interior of this easy-to-bake bread is delicious and a great addition to the menu as a snack or side, with dips or classic balsamic and olive oil.

basic flatbread dough

2 teaspoons active dry yeast*
1 teaspoon caster (superfine) sugar
1⅓ cup (80ml) lukewarm milk
2½ cups (375g) plain (all-purpose) flour
1 teaspoon table salt
1 tablespoon olive oil, and extra,
for brushing
sea salt flakes, for sprinkling

step 1

step 2

step 1 Place the yeast, sugar and milk in a bowl and mix to combine. Set aside in a warm place for 5 minutes or until bubbles appear on the surface.

step 2 Preheat oven to 180°C (350°F). Place the flour, table salt, oil and yeast mixture in a bowl and mix until a smooth dough forms. Knead on a lightly floured surface for 5 minutes or until smooth and elastic, adding a little extra flour to the dough if it is sticky. Return to the bowl, cover with a tea towel and set aside in a warm place for 30 minutes or until dough has doubled in size.

step 3 Press dough into a lightly greased 26cm-round baking tray to 1cm-thick, brush with oil and sprinkle with salt. Bake for 15–20 minutes or until golden. *Serves 6.*

recipe notes
ON THE RISE
When pressing the dough into a tray, it's best to start spreading it from the centre and gently pushing it towards the edges of the tray. Simply brush the surface with olive oil, sprinkle with sea salt and pop in the oven. With the dough spread evenly, the heat will be distributed so it will rise equally across the tray.

cook's tip
Flatbread is best eaten still warm from the oven or on the day it is baked. If you need to reheat, preheat the oven to 180°C (350°F), wrap the bread in aluminium foil and heat until warm.

chilli and anchovy flatbread

1 x quantity basic flatbread dough (see recipe, page 68)
olive oil, for brushing
½ cup (85g) pitted black olives
10 anchovy fillets
½ teaspoon dried chilli flakes
1 teaspoon thyme leaves
sea salt flakes, for sprinkling

Preheat oven to 180°C (350°F). Follow steps 1 and 2 of the basic dough recipe. Press the dough into a 26cm-round lightly greased baking tray, brush with oil and top with olives, anchovies, chilli, thyme and sprinkle with salt. Bake for 20 minutes or until golden. *Serves 6.*

fennel and coriander rolls

1 teaspoon fennel seeds
1 teaspoon sesame seeds
1 teaspoon cumin seeds
1 teaspoon coriander (cilantro) seeds
½ teaspoon sea salt flakes
1 x quantity basic flatbread dough (see recipe, page 68)
olive oil, for brushing

Place the fennel, sesame, cumin, coriander and salt in a small food processor and process until roughly chopped. Set aside.

Preheat oven to 180°C (350°F). Follow steps 1 and 2 of the basic dough recipe. Divide into 12 equal-sized portions and roll into balls. Brush 12 x ½ cup-capacity (125ml) muffin tins with oil and sprinkle with half the fennel mixture. Place a ball of dough in each muffin tin, brush with oil and sprinkle with remaining fennel mixture. Bake for 20–25 minutes or until golden. *Makes 12.*

garlic and rosemary oil flatbread

1 x quantity basic flatbread dough (see recipe, page 68)
3 tablespoons olive oil
¼ cup rosemary leaves
2 cloves garlic, crushed
1 cup (80g) finely grated parmesan
sea salt flakes

Preheat oven to 180°C (350°F). Follow steps 1 and 2 of the basic dough recipe. Place the oil, rosemary and garlic in a bowl and allow to stand for 10–15 minutes. Press the dough into a 25cm x 35cm lightly greased baking tray, brush with the olive oil mixture and sprinkle with parmesan and salt. Use a small knife to make cuts across the dough. Bake for 15–20 minutes or until golden. *Serves 6.*

caramelised eschalot and goat's cheese flatbread

15 eschalots (French shallots)*, peeled and halved
2 tablespoons olive oil
2 tablespoons brown sugar
1 x quantity basic flatbread dough (see recipe, page 68)
100g goat's cheese, crumbled
olive oil, extra, for brushing
basil oil
⅓ cup (60ml) olive oil
1 cup basil leaves

Preheat oven to 180°C (350°F). To make the basil oil, place the oil and basil in a small food processor and process until well combined. Set aside.

Place the eschalots, oil and sugar in a bowl and toss to coat. Place in a baking dish and roast for 15–20 minutes or until golden and caramelised. Set aside.

Follow steps 1 and 2 of the basic dough recipe. After the dough has doubled in size, add the goat's cheese and mix well to combine. Press the dough into a 20cm x 30cm lightly greased baking tray, brush with oil and top with the eschalots. Bake for 15–20 minutes or until golden. Brush with the basil oil to serve. *Serves 6.*

baking

sponge cake

pound cake

chocolate cake

shortcrust pastry

caramel slice

vanilla cupcakes

scones

choux pastry

blueberry muffins

shortbread

brioche

sponge cake

A heavenly light and fluffy sponge cake filled with jam and cream is a classic treat — or try one of these simple variations for something a little more special.

step 1

step 2

step 3

basic sponge cake

⅔ cup (100g) plain (all-purpose) flour
¼ teaspoon baking powder
4 eggs
½ cup (110g) caster (superfine) sugar
50g butter, melted
1 cup (320g) strawberry jam (jelly)
1 cup (250ml) single (pouring) cream, whipped
icing (confectioner's) sugar, to serve

step 1 Preheat oven to 180°C (350°F). Sift the flour and baking powder three times. Set aside.

step 2 Place the eggs and sugar in the bowl of an electric mixer and beat for 8–10 minutes or until the mixture is thick, pale and tripled in volume.

step 3 Sift half the flour mixture over the egg mixture and gently fold through. Repeat with the remaining flour. Add the butter and fold through. Divide the mixture between 2 lightly greased, shallow 19cm-round cake tins lined with non-stick baking paper and bake for 20–25 minutes or until the sponges are springy to the touch and come away from the sides of the tin. Remove from the tins and place on wire racks to cool.

step 4 Spread 1 sponge with jam, top with the cream and sandwich with remaining sponge. Dust with icing sugar to serve. *Serves 6–8.*

recipe notes

sift – Sponges take their light and fluffy texture from an aerated mixture; sifting the flour and baking powder three times will ensure your sponge has sufficient air.
beat – To add more air to your sponge, make sure to beat the eggs and sugar until the mixture has tripled in volume.
fold – Using a large metal spoon to fold the butter through the flour and egg will help to leave the air bubbles intact.
feel – Never use a skewer to check your sponge is cooked, as it will release the precious air. If the sponge is springy to touch and comes away from the sides of the tin, it's ready.

caramel and brown sugar sponge cake

⅔ cup (100g) plain (all-purpose) flour, sifted 3 times
½ teaspoon baking powder, sifted 3 times
4 eggs
¼ cup (45g) brown sugar
¼ cup (55g) caster (superfine) sugar
50g butter, melted
caramel icing
1 cup (175g) brown sugar
1 cup (250ml) single (pouring) cream

To make the caramel icing, place the sugar and cream in a small saucepan over medium heat and stir until the sugar is dissolved. Increase the heat to high and cook for 8 minutes or until the caramel thickens. Allow to cool completely.

Preheat oven to 180°C (350°F). Place the flour and baking powder in a bowl. Place the eggs and sugar in an electric mixer and beat for 8–10 minutes or until thick, pale and tripled in volume. Sift half the flour mixture over the egg mixture and gently fold through. Repeat with remaining flour. Add the butter and fold through. Pour into a lightly greased 20cm-round cake tin lined with non-stick baking paper and bake for 20–25 minutes or until springy to the touch and coming away from the sides of the tin. Cool on a wire rack. Spread cake with the caramel icing to serve. *Serves 6–8.*

coffee sponge cakes with mascarpone

⅔ cup (100g) plain (all-purpose) flour, sifted 3 times
¼ teaspoon baking powder, sifted 3 times
4 eggs
½ cup (110g) caster (superfine) sugar
50g butter, melted
1 tablespoon each instant coffee and hot water
¼ cup (60ml) coffee-flavoured liqueur
mascarpone icing
250g mascarpone
1 tablespoon brown sugar

To make the mascarpone icing, place the mascarpone and brown sugar in a bowl and whisk until just combined. Set aside.

Preheat oven to 180°C (350°F). Place the flour and baking powder in a bowl. Place the eggs and sugar in an electric mixer and beat for 8–10 minutes or until thick, pale and tripled in volume. Sift half the flour mixture over the egg mixture and fold through. Repeat with remaining flour and add the butter. Dissolve the coffee in the water and fold through. Divide between 8 x ¾ cup-capacity (180ml) lightly greased muffin tins and bake for 20–25 minutes or until springy to the touch. Cool on wire racks. Spoon over the liqueur and top with mascarpone icing to serve. *Makes 8.*

chocolate sponge kisses with strawberries

⅓ cup (50g) plain (all-purpose) flour, sifted 3 times
¼ teaspoon baking powder, sifted 3 times
⅓ cup (35g) cocoa, sifted 3 times
4 eggs
½ cup (110g) caster (superfine) sugar
50g butter, melted
1 cup (250ml) thick (double) cream, lightly whipped
1 cup sliced strawberries
icing (confectioner's) sugar, to serve

Preheat oven to 180°C (350°F). Place the flour, baking powder and cocoa in a bowl. Set aside.

Place the eggs and sugar in an electric mixer and beat for 8–10 minutes or until thick, pale and tripled in volume. Sift half the flour mixture over the egg mixture and gently fold through. Repeat with the remaining flour. Add the butter and gently fold through. Place tablespoonfuls of the mixture on baking trays lined with non-stick baking paper and bake for 8–10 minutes or until puffed. Cool on wire racks. To assemble, spread the kisses with the cream, top half with strawberry slices and sandwich with the remaining kisses. Dust with the icing sugar to serve. *Makes 10.*

upside-down rhubarb sponge

⅔ cup (100g) plain (all-purpose) flour, sifted 3 times
¼ teaspoon baking powder, sifted 3 times
4 eggs
½ cup (110g) caster (superfine) sugar
50g butter, melted
rhubarb topping
450g rhubarb, trimmed and cut into 21cm lengths
¼ cup (45g) brown sugar
1 teaspoon vanilla extract

To make the rhubarb topping, place the rhubarb, brown sugar and vanilla in a bowl and toss to combine. Set aside.

Preheat oven to 180°C (350°F). Place the flour and baking powder in a bowl. Place the eggs and sugar in an electric mixer and beat for 8–10 minutes or until thick, pale and tripled in volume. Sift half the flour mixture over the egg mixture and gently fold through. Repeat with the remaining flour. Add the butter and gently fold through. Place the rhubarb mixture in the base of a lightly greased, shallow 22cm-square cake tin lined with non-stick baking paper and pour over the cake mixture. Bake for 20–25 minutes or until springy to the touch and coming away from the sides of the tin. Carefully turn the cake upside down and remove from the tin. Cool on a wire rack. *Serves 6–8.*

caramel and brown sugar sponge cake

chocolate sponge kisses with strawberries

coffee sponge cakes with mascarpone

upside-down rhubarb sponge

pound cake

Rich and delicious pound cake with its equal quantities of butter, sugar and flour is easy to remember and is sure to become a favourite stand-by treat.

step 1

step 2

pound cake

250g butter, softened
250g caster (superfine) sugar
1 teaspoon vanilla extract
4 eggs
250g plain (all-purpose) flour, sifted
¼ cup (60ml) milk

step 1 Preheat oven to 160°C (325°F). Place the butter, sugar and vanilla in the bowl of an electric mixer and beat for 10–12 minutes or until light and creamy.

step 2 Add the eggs, one at a time, beating well after each addition. Add the flour and beat well to combine. Fold through the milk. Spoon the mixture into a lightly greased 20cm round cake tin lined with non-stick baking paper and bake for 45–50 minutes or until cooked when tested with a skewer. Allow to cool in the tin. *Serves 8–10.*

try this...

RASPBERRY CAKES
Follow the basic recipe, folding through 1 cup (125g) frozen raspberries with the milk at step 2. Spoon into 8 x ¾ cup-capacity (180ml) lightly greased muffin tins and bake for 25–30 minutes or until cooked when tested with a skewer. Cool in tins. Dust with icing sugar to serve.

CHOCOLATE CHIP POUND CAKE
Follow the basic recipe, folding through ¾ cup (135g) chopped dark chocolate with the milk at step 2. Bake for 50–55 minutes or until cooked when tested with a skewer. Cool in tin. Dust with cocoa to serve.

recipe notes

The generous butter content adds to the moistness and volume of the cake and needs to be at room temperature for the mixture to become light and creamy. Adding and beating in the eggs one at a time binds the ingredients together and aerates the mixture to help the cake rise.

chocolate cake

250g butter
1⅓ cups (235g) brown sugar
3 eggs
2 cups (300g) plain (all-purpose) flour
1½ teaspoons baking powder
⅓ cup (35g) cocoa, sifted
1 cup (240g) sour cream
250g dark chocolate, melted
chocolate glaze
150g dark chocolate, chopped
⅓ cup (80ml) single (pouring) cream

step 1 Preheat oven to 160°C (325°F). Place the butter and sugar in the bowl of an electric mixer and beat until light and creamy. Add the eggs and beat well. Sift the flour, baking powder and cocoa over the butter mixture, add the sour cream and chocolate and mix until just combined. Pour the mixture into a lightly greased 22cm-round cake tin lined with non-stick baking paper and bake for 60–70 minutes or until just set. Allow to cool in tin.

step 2 While the cake is baking, make the chocolate glaze. Place the chocolate and cream in a small saucepan over low heat and stir until melted and smooth. Allow glaze to stand for 10 minutes to thicken slightly before spreading over the cake. *Serves 8–10.*

icing on the top
CHOCOLATE FUDGE ICING
Place 250g dark chocolate, ½ cup (125ml) single (pouring) cream and 70g butter in a heatproof bowl over a saucepan of simmering water and stir until melted and smooth. Remove from heat and set aside to cool completely. Once cooled, beat with a hand-held electric beater until thick and fluffy.

VANILLA CREAM FROSTING
Place 250g softened butter in the bowl of an electric mixer and beat until light and creamy. Add 1 cup (160g) sifted icing (confectioner's) sugar and 1 teaspoon vanilla extract and beat until well combined.

step 1   step 2

shortcrust pastry

A little time and effort is all it takes to make your own pastry. With its beautifully buttery flavour and decadent texture it turns homemade tarts into a special indulgence.

step 3

step 4

basic sweet shortcrust pastry

1½ cups (225g) plain (all-purpose) flour
125g butter, chilled and cut into cubes
½ cup (80g) icing (confectioner's) sugar
3 egg yolks
1 tablespoon iced water

step 1 Place the flour, butter and sugar in the bowl of a food processor and process in short bursts until the mixture resembles fine breadcrumbs.

step 2 While the motor is running, add the egg yolks and water. Process until the dough just comes together. Turn dough out onto a lightly floured surface and gently bring together to form a ball. Using your hands, flatten dough into a disk. Wrap in plastic wrap and refrigerate for 1 hour.

step 3 Preheat oven to 180°C (350°F). Roll dough out between 2 sheets of non-stick baking paper to 3mm thick. Once rolled, you may need to refrigerate to chill (see recipe notes, below). Line a lightly greased 22cm loose-bottomed tart tin with the pastry. Trim edges and prick the base with a fork. Refrigerate for 30 minutes.

step 4 Line the pastry case with non-stick baking paper and fill with baking weights. Bake for 15 minutes, remove the paper and weights and cook for a further 10 minutes or until the pastry is light golden. Allow to cool in the tin. Fill with your favourite filling to serve. Serves 6–8.

recipe notes

Shortcrust pastry owes its 'short', crisp texture to butter. The butter can make the pastry quite soft and difficult to roll. If you find your pastry is too soft at any stage, pop it in the fridge for a few minutes to firm up.

frangipane and lemon tart

1 x quantity basic sweet shortcrust pastry (see recipe, page 80)
1 teaspoon finely grated lemon rind
100g butter, softened
½ cup (110g) caster (superfine) sugar
1 egg
1 egg yolk, extra
1 cup (120g) almond meal (ground almonds)*
¼ cup (35g) plain (all-purpose) flour
¼ cup (20g) flaked almonds

Make the basic sweet shortcrust pastry, adding the lemon rind
at step 1.
   Place the butter and sugar in the bowl of an electric mixer and
beat until light and creamy. Gradually add the egg and extra egg
yolk and beat until just combined. Stir through the almond meal
and flour until well combined. Spoon mixture into the pastry case
and top with the flaked almonds. Bake for 30–35 minutes or until
the frangipane has set. Allow to cool in the tin. *Serves 6–8.*

coconut and lemon curd tarts

1 x quantity basic sweet shortcrust pastry (see recipe, page 80)
½ cup (25g) flaked coconut
¾ cup (300g) store-bought lemon curd (or see recipe, page 114)
fresh raspberries, to serve
icing (confectioner's) sugar, for dusting

Make the basic sweet shortcrust pastry, adding the coconut at step 1.
At step 3, line 4 x 12cm x 7cm lightly greased loose-bottomed tart
tins with the pastry.
   Place the lemon curd in a bowl and whisk until smooth. Spoon
into the pastry cases and refrigerate for 1–2 hours. Top the lemon
curd with raspberries and dust with icing sugar to serve. *Serves 4.*

chocolate ganache tart

1 x quantity basic sweet shortcrust pastry (see recipe, page 80)
¼ cup (25g) cocoa
300g dark chocolate, chopped
1 cup (250ml) single (pouring) cream

Make the basic sweet shortcrust pastry, adding the cocoa at step 1. At step 3, line a 34cm x 10cm lightly greased loose-bottomed tart tin with the pastry.

Place the chocolate and cream in a small saucepan over low heat and stir until melted and smooth. Allow mixture to stand for 10 minutes or until thickened slightly. Pour the chocolate mixture into the pastry shell and gently tap to remove any air bubbles. Refrigerate for 1-2 hours or until set. *Serves 6-8.*

mascarpone and rhubarb cinnamon tart

1 x quantity basic sweet shortcrust pastry (see recipe, page 80)
1 teaspoon ground cinnamon
16 x 10cm rhubarb pieces
2 tablespoons caster (superfine) sugar
1 tablespoon water
1½ cups (350g) mascarpone
¾ cup (180ml) single (pouring) cream
¼ cup (40g) icing (confectioner's) sugar
½ teaspoon vanilla extract

Make the basic sweet shortcrust pastry, adding the cinnamon at step 1. At step 3, line 4 x 8cm round lightly greased loose-bottom tart tins with the pastry.

Combine the rhubarb, caster sugar and water in a bowl. Place on a tray lined with non-stick baking paper, cover with foil and bake for 15-20 minutes or until tender. Set aside to cool.

Place the mascarpone, cream, icing sugar and vanilla in a bowl and mix to combine. Spoon into the pastry shells. Top tarts with the rhubarb and drizzle with rhubarb juices to serve. *Serves 4.*

caramel slice

1 cup (150g) plain (all-purpose) flour, sifted
½ cup (40g) desiccated coconut
½ cup (90g) brown sugar
125g butter, melted
caramel filling
⅓ cup (115g) golden syrup
125g butter, chopped
2 x 395g cans sweetened condensed milk
chocolate topping
200g dark chocolate, chopped
1 tablespoon vegetable oil

step 1 Preheat oven to 180°C (350°F). Place the flour, coconut, sugar and butter in a bowl and mix well to combine. Using the back of a spoon, press into the base of a lightly greased 20cm x 30cm tin lined with non-stick baking paper and bake for 20–25 minutes or until golden.

step 2 While the base is cooking, make the caramel filling. Place the golden syrup, butter and condensed milk in a saucepan over low heat and cook for 6–7 minutes, stirring continuously, or until butter has melted and caramel has thickened slightly. Pour over the cooked base and bake for 20 minutes or until golden. Refrigerate until cold.

step 3 To make the chocolate topping, place the chocolate and oil in a heatproof bowl over a saucepan of simmering water and stir until melted and smooth. Pour over the caramel mixture and refrigerate for 30 minutes or until firm. *Makes 15.*

step 1   step 2

cook's tip

When cutting slices with a chocolate topping or a soft and sticky filling, dip your knife into hot water and dry with a tea towel before slicing. The warm knife will then make a clean cut and ensure neat slices.

vanilla cupcakes

No matter what their age, everyone loves a cupcake. Simply add your favourite icing or fun decorations to top off these sweet, hand-held delights.

step 1   step 2

vanilla cupcakes

1¼ cups (185g) plain (all-purpose)
flour, sifted
¾ teaspoon baking powder, sifted
1 cup (220g) caster (superfine) sugar
125g butter, softened
2 eggs
¾ cups (180ml) milk
½ teaspoon vanilla extract

step 1 Preheat oven to 160°C (325°F). Place the flour, baking powder, sugar, butter, eggs, milk and vanilla in the bowl of an electric mixer and mix to combine.

step 2 Spoon into 12 x ½ cup-capacity (125ml) muffin tins lined with paper cases and bake for 20–25 minutes or until cooked when tested with a skewer. Cool on wire racks. Ice as desired. *Makes 12.*

try this...
LEMON ICING
Place 1½ cups (240g) sifted icing (confectioner's) sugar, 2 tablespoons water, 2 tablespoons lemon juice and 1 teaspoon finely grated lemon rind in a bowl and mix until smooth. You could also make orange or lime icing by replacing the lemon juice and rind with orange or lime juice and rind.

decorating tips
You can make fun cupcakes for kids by topping with icing and lollies - you're only limited by your imagination. Spread basic cupcakes with the vanilla cream frosting (page 79) and decorate with your favourite lollies, such as coloured sprinkles and candy-coated chocolates. You can even add a few drops of food colouring to the icing for fun colours.

scones

This classic accompaniment to a cup of tea is simple to make and is an essential for every cook's repertoire. All you need is a feather-light touch for perfect scones every time.

basic scones

3 cups (450g) self-raising (self-rising)
flour, sifted
½ cup (110g) caster (superfine) sugar
75g cold butter, chopped
1 cup (250ml) milk, plus extra, for brushing
raspberry jam, to serve
chantilly cream
¾ cup (180ml) single (pouring) cream
¼ cup (40g) icing (confectioner's) sugar,
sifted

step 1

step 3

step 1 Preheat oven to 180°C (350°F). Place the flour and sugar in a bowl and mix to combine. Add the butter and use your fingertips to rub it into the flour mixture until it resembles fine breadcrumbs.

step 2 Make a well in the centre and pour in the milk. Use a butter knife to gradually mix the milk into the flour mixture until just combined.

step 3 Turn out onto a lightly floured surface and gently bring the dough

together (see *cook's tips*). Roll dough out to 2cm thick and use a 6cm-round cutter to cut 12 rounds. Place the scones on a lightly greased baking tray lined with non-stick baking paper and brush with extra milk. Bake for 18–20 minutes or until cooked when tested with a skewer.

step 4 To make the chantilly cream, place the cream and icing sugar in a bowl and whisk until soft peaks form. Serve scones with cream and raspberry jam. *Makes 12.*

cook's tips
The most important thing to remember when making scones is not to overwork the dough or you'll end up with a hard, tough scone. By using a butter knife to mix the dough and bringing it lightly together with your hands, you avoid overworking the gluten in the dough. Using very cold butter will ensure a deliciously flaky texture.

coconut jam scones

raspberry and almond scone

chocolate swirl scone loaf

date and orange scones

chocolate swirl scone loaf

1½ cups (225g) self-raising (self-rising) flour, sifted
¼ cup (55g) caster (superfine) sugar
40g cold butter, chopped
½ cup (125ml) milk, plus extra, for brushing
100g dark chocolate, finely chopped

Preheat oven to 180°C (350°F). Place the flour and sugar in a bowl and mix to combine. Add the butter and use your fingertips to rub it into the flour mixture until it resembles fine breadcrumbs. Make a well in the centre and pour in the milk. Use a butter knife to gradually mix the milk into the flour mixture until just combined. Turn out onto a lightly floured surface and gently bring the dough together. Roll out to a 18cm x 24cm rectangle. Sprinkle with the chocolate and roll to enclose. Place in a lightly greased 19cm x 9cm loaf tin lined with non-stick baking paper. Brush with extra milk and bake for 25–30 minutes or until cooked when tested with a skewer. Cool in the tin for 5 minutes and then turn out on to a wire rack to cool. Slice to serve. *Serves 6–8.*

raspberry and almond scone

1½ cups (225g) self-raising (self-rising) flour, sifted
½ cup (110g) caster (superfine) sugar
40g cold butter, chopped
¾ cup (120g) frozen raspberries
2 teaspoons caster (superfine) sugar, extra
½ cup (125ml) milk, plus extra, for brushing
1 tablespoon flaked almonds
icing (confectioner's) sugar, for dusting

Preheat oven to 180°C (350°F). Place the flour and sugar in a bowl and mix to combine. Add the butter and use your fingertips to rub it into the flour mixture until it resembles fine breadcrumbs. Place the raspberries and extra sugar in a bowl and toss to combine. Stir ¼ cup of the raspberry mixture through the flour mixture. Make a well in the centre and pour in the milk. Use a butter knife to gradually mix the milk into the flour mixture until just combined. Turn out onto a lightly floured surface and gently bring the dough together. Shape into a 16cm round and place on a lightly greased baking tray lined with non-stick baking paper. Score the top of the scone with a knife and brush with extra milk. Press the remaining raspberries into the top of the scone and sprinkle with the almonds. Bake for 25 minutes or until cooked when tested with a skewer. Dust with icing sugar to serve. *Serves 6.*

date and orange scones

3 cups (450g) self-raising (self-rising) flour, sifted
½ cup (110g) caster (superfine) sugar
1 tablespoon finely grated orange rind
75g cold butter, chopped
1 cup (70g) chopped pitted dates
1 cup (250ml) milk, plus extra, for brushing
raw sugar, for sprinkling
butter, extra, to serve

Preheat oven to 180°C (350°F). Place the flour, sugar and orange rind in a bowl and mix to combine. Add the butter and use your fingertips to rub it into the flour mixture until it resembles fine breadcrumbs. Stir the dates through the flour mixture. Make a well in the centre and pour in the milk. Use a butter knife to gradually mix the milk into the flour mixture until just combined. Turn out onto a lightly floured surface and gently bring the dough together. Roll out to 2cm thick and use a 6cm-round cutter to cut 16 rounds. Place the scones together on a lightly greased baking tray lined with non-stick baking paper and brush with extra milk. Sprinkle with raw sugar and bake for 18–20 minutes or until cooked when tested with a skewer. Serve with butter. *Makes 16.*

coconut jam scones

3 cups (450g) self-raising (self-rising) flour, sifted
½ cup (110g) caster (superfine) sugar
¾ cup (60g) desiccated coconut
75g cold butter, chopped
1 cup (250ml) milk, plus extra, for brushing
½ cup (160g) blackberry, strawberry or raspberry jam
raw sugar, for sprinkling

Preheat oven to 180°C (350°F). Place the flour, sugar and coconut in a bowl and mix to combine. Add the butter and use your fingertips to rub it into the flour mixture until it resembles fine breadcrumbs. Make a well in the centre and pour in the milk. Use a butter knife to gradually mix the milk into the flour mixture until just combined. Turn out onto a lightly floured surface and gently bring the dough together. Halve the dough and roll each piece out to a 35cm x 20cm rectangle, 1cm thick. Spread one of the pieces with the jam and sandwich with remaining piece of dough. Use a 6cm round cutter to cut out 12 rounds. Place the scones in 12 x ½ cup-capacity (125ml) muffin tins lined with paper cases. Brush with extra milk and sprinkle with raw sugar. Bake for 18–20 minutes or until cooked when tested with a skewer. *Makes 12.*

choux pastry

Don't be daunted by this elegant and airy French delight,
it only takes a few simple steps to be rewarded with a plate
brimming with irresistible and ever-so-chic pastries.

basic choux pastries

½ cup (125ml) water
50g butter
½ cup (75g) plain (all-purpose) flour
3 eggs
1 cup (250ml) store-bought custard
icing (confectioner's) sugar, for dusting

step 1

step 2

step 1 Preheat oven to 180°C (350°F).
Place the water and butter in a medium
saucepan over high heat and cook until
butter is melted and the mixture is boiling.
Add the flour and beat with a wooden
spoon until smooth.

step 2 Cook, stirring over low heat, until
the mixture leaves the sides of the pan.
Remove from heat and place in an electric
mixer. Gradually add eggs, beating well
between each addition, until well combined.

Spoon the mixture into a piping bag with
a 1cm plain nozzle. Pipe 4cm rounds onto
baking trays lined with non-stick baking
paper, allowing space to spread. Bake for
30-35 minutes or until puffed and golden.
Cool on wire racks.

step 3 Using a small nozzle[+] on a piping
bag, pipe custard into the base of each
profiterole until full. Dust with icing sugar
to serve. *Makes 16.*

*+ Use a nozzle with a small width to avoid
creating a large hole in the pastry. Gently
push into the base of the pastry to fill.*

recipe notes

Use a wooden spoon and your arm strength to vigorously beat
the flour into the butter mixture until it comes away from
the sides of the pan. When adding the eggs, beat well between
each addition. It will initially look as though the egg is
separated from the mixture, so it's important the mixture
is smooth before adding the next egg. If, when you lift up
the beater, you can see ribbons form on the surface of the
mixture, the eggs are well combined.

raspberry ice-cream choux sandwiches

½ cup (125ml) water
50g butter
½ cup (75g) plain (all-purpose) flour
3 eggs
2 cups (500ml) store-bought raspberry ice-cream

Preheat oven to 180°C (350°F). Place the water and butter in a medium saucepan over high heat and cook until butter is melted and the mixture is boiling. Add the flour and beat with a wooden spoon until smooth. Cook, stirring over low heat, until the mixture leaves the sides of the pan. Remove from heat and place in an electric mixer. Gradually add eggs, beating well between each addition, until well combined.

Spoon mixture into a piping bag with a 1cm plain nozzle. Pipe 4cm rounds onto trays lined with non-stick baking paper. Bake for 20-25 minutes or until puffed and golden. Cool on wire racks.

To assemble, cut the profiteroles in half horizontally, spoon ice-cream onto the base of profiteroles and sandwich with the remaining profiterole tops. *Makes 16.*

chocolate éclairs

½ cup (125ml) water
50g butter
½ cup (75g) plain (all-purpose) flour
3 eggs
200g dark chocolate, chopped
1 teaspoon vegetable oil
½ cup (125ml) single (pouring) cream
1 tablespoon icing (confectioner's) sugar
1 teaspoon vanilla essence

Preheat oven to 180°C (350°F). Place the water and butter in a medium saucepan over high heat and cook until butter is melted and the mixture is boiling. Add the flour and beat with a wooden spoon until smooth. Cook, stirring over low heat, until the mixture leaves the sides of the pan. Remove from heat and place in an electric mixer. Gradually add eggs, beating well between each addition, until well combined.

Spoon mixture into a piping bag with a 1cm plain nozzle. Pipe 7cm lengths onto trays lined with non-stick baking paper. Bake for 20-25 minutes or until puffed and golden. Cool on wire racks.

Place the chocolate and oil in a heatproof bowl over a saucepan of simmering water and stir until chocolate is melted and smooth.

Place cream, icing sugar and vanilla in a bowl and whisk until soft peaks form. To assemble, use a small, sharp knife to make a horizontal cut in the profiteroles, pipe cream into the centre. Dip profiterole tops in melted chocolate and allow to set. *Makes 8.*

cinnamon-sugar puffs

½ cup (125ml) water
50g butter
½ cup (75g) plain (all-purpose) flour
3 eggs
vegetable oil, for deep-frying
1½ cups (330g) caster (superfine) sugar
2 teaspoons cinnamon

Preheat oven to 180°C (350°F). Place the water and butter in a medium saucepan over high heat and cook until butter is melted and the mixture is boiling. Add the flour and beat with a wooden spoon until smooth. Cook, stirring over low heat, until the mixture leaves the sides of the pan. Remove from heat and place in the bowl of an electric mixer. Gradually add eggs, beating well between each addition, until well combined.

Heat oil in a large, deep saucepan over medium heat until hot. Drop one teaspoon of dough into the oil at a time and cook, in batches, for 3-4 minutes or until golden and puffed. Mix sugar and cinnamon to combine. Roll the puffs in cinnamon sugar and serve immediately. *Makes 24.*

lemon cream profiteroles

½ cup (125ml) water
50g butter
½ cup (75g) plain (all-purpose) flour
3 eggs
½ cup (125ml) single (pouring) cream, whipped
½ cup (175g) store-bought lemon curd (or see recipe, page 114)
icing (confectioner's) sugar, for dusting

Preheat oven to 180°C (350°F). Place the water and butter in a medium saucepan over high heat and cook until butter is melted and the mixture is boiling. Add the flour and beat with a wooden spoon until smooth. Cook, stirring over low heat, until the mixture leaves the sides of the pan. Remove from heat and place in an electric mixer. Gradually add eggs, beating well between each addition, until well combined.

Spoon the mixture into a piping bag with a 1cm plain nozzle. Pipe 5cm rounds onto baking trays lined with non-stick baking paper. Bake for 20-25 minutes or until puffed and golden. Cool on wire racks.

Place cream and curd in a bowl and gently fold to combine.

To assemble, cut the profiteroles in half horizontally, spoon the lemon cream onto the base of the profiteroles and sandwich with remaining tops. Dust with icing sugar to serve. *Makes 12.*

raspberry ice-cream choux sandwiches

cinnamon-sugar puffs

lemon cream profiteroles

chocolate éclairs

blueberry muffins

If they're not gobbled up within minutes of leaving the oven, these golden muffins studded with juicy blueberries make for great lunchbox or picnic treats.

step 2   step 3

blueberry muffins

2 cups (300g) plain (all-purpose)
flour, sifted
2 teaspoons baking powder, sifted
¾ cup (165g) caster (superfine) sugar
1 cup (240g) sour cream
2 eggs
1 teaspoon finely grated lemon rind
⅓ cup (80ml) vegetable oil
1¼ cup (190g) fresh or frozen blueberries

step 1 Preheat oven to 180°C (350°F). Place the flour, baking powder and sugar in a bowl and stir to combine.

step 2 Place the sour cream, eggs, lemon rind and oil in a bowl and whisk until smooth. Add the sour cream mixture to the flour mixture and stir until just combined.

step 3 Sprinkle over the blueberries and stir once. Spoon the mixture into 12 x ½ cup-capacity (125ml) non-stick muffin tins and bake for 12 minutes or until cooked when tested with a skewer. *Makes 12.*

try this…

RASPBERRY AND WHITE CHOCOLATE MUFFINS
Omit the lemon rind from the basic recipe. Replace the blueberries with raspberries and add ¾ cup (135g) chopped white chocolate at step 2.

BANANA AND CINNAMON MUFFINS
Add 1 teaspoon ground cinnamon with the flour at step 1 and replace the blueberries with 1 cup chopped banana.

shortbread

250g cold butter, chopped
1 cup (160g) icing (confectioner's) sugar, sifted
1½ cups (225g) plain (all-purpose) flour, sifted
½ cup (100g) rice flour++, sifted
1 teaspoon vanilla extract
icing (confectioner's) sugar, extra, for dusting

step 1 Preheat oven to 180°C (350°F). Place butter, icing sugar, plain flour, rice flour and vanilla in the bowl of a food processor and process until the dough just comes together.

step 2 Lightly grease a 24cm-round loose-bottomed fluted tin. Press dough into tin using the back of a spoon. Refrigerate for 15 minutes or until firm. Use a 6cm round cookie cutter to cut a round from the centre of the dough++. Discard the round and place the cutter back in the centre. Use a sharp knife to score the dough into 8 wedges and prick with a skewer.

step 3 Bake for 35–40 minutes or until light golden. Remove from the tin and allow to cool on a wire rack. Dust with icing sugar and cut into wedges to serve. *Serves 8.*

+ *Rice flour gives shortbread its classic crisp, crumbly texture.*
++ *Removing a round from the centre creates a more traditional shortbread shape. It also prevents the end of the biscuit from breaking off, as it removes the fragile point.*

step 1

step 2

cook's tips

smooth – Pressing the dough into the tin with the back of a spoon will help to give your shortbread a smooth, even surface.
score – Use a sharp knife to score the uncooked dough as this will make it easier to cut once cooked.

brioche

Rich and decadent, this classic, buttery French bread is
a real crowd-pleaser and is worth the proving time — the
heavenly result will have everyone asking for seconds.

step 1

step 3

step 4

basic brioche

1 x 8g sachet dry yeast*
1 tablespoon lukewarm water
¼ cup (55g) caster (superfine) sugar
¼ teaspoon sea salt flakes
2 tablespoons lukewarm milk
1⅔ cups (250g) OO flour*
2 eggs, lightly beaten
225g butter, chopped and softened
1 egg, extra, lightly beaten

step 1 Place the yeast and water in a
bowl and mix to combine. Set aside in a
warm place for 5 minutes or until bubbles
appear on the surface. Combine the sugar,
salt and milk in a separate bowl. Place the
flour, yeast mixture and egg in the bowl of
an electric mixer and, using a dough hook,
beat on low for 1 minute. Increase speed
to high, add the milk mixture and beat for
10 minutes or until dough comes away
from the sides of the bowl.

step 2 While the motor is running,
gradually add the butter and beat for
6-7 minutes or until glossy and elastic.

step 3 Place the dough in a bowl and
cover with plastic wrap. Set aside in a
warm place for 2-3 hours or until the
dough has doubled in size.

step 4 Divide the dough into 4 equal-
size balls and knead on a lightly floured
surface until smooth. Place in a 22cm x 8cm
lightly greased loaf tin, cover with a clean,
damp cloth and set aside for 1 hour or until
doubled in size. Preheat oven to 180°C
(350°F). Make a cut in the centre of each
ball, brush with the extra egg and bake for
35-40 minutes or until golden. Allow to
stand for 10 minutes. *Serves 8.*

recipe notes

The amount of butter in the dough results in a deliciously
golden brioche, but it can also make the dough very sticky.
To avoid the dough becoming difficult to work with, it is a
good idea to roll it out on a cool, lightly floured benchtop.

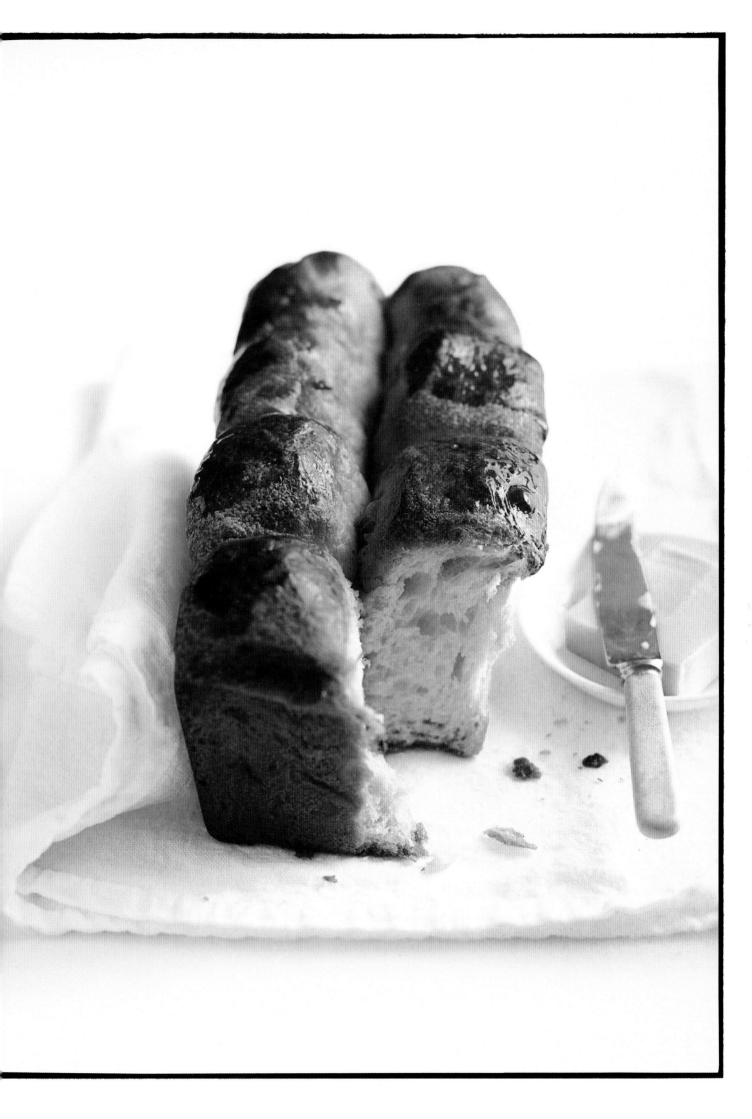

cinnamon brioche scrolls

1 x quantity basic brioche dough (see recipe, page 96)
¼ cup (55g) caster (superfine) sugar
½ tablespoon ground cinnamon
1 egg, lightly beaten
1½ tablespoons Demerara sugar*

Make the basic brioche dough, following steps 1, 2 and 3. Place the caster sugar and cinnamon in a bowl and mix well to combine. Roll the dough out on a lightly floured surface to a 45cm x 25cm rectangle. Sprinkle the dough with the cinnamon mixture and starting from the longest edge, roll to enclose filling. Using a sharp knife, trim the edges and cut into 14 pieces. Place scrolls side by side in a 20cm round lightly greased tin, cover with a clean, damp cloth and set aside for 1 hour or until dough has doubled in size.

Preheat oven to 180°C (350°F). Brush the dough with egg and sprinkle with the Demerara sugar. Bake for 15 minutes, loosely cover with aluminium foil and bake for a further 15–20 minutes or until golden. Turn out onto a wire rack to cool. *Makes 14.*

orange brioche muffins with lemon icing

1 x quantity basic brioche dough (see recipe, page 96)
1 tablespoon finely grated orange rind
1 egg, lightly beaten
shredded orange zest, to serve
lemon icing
2 cups (320g) icing (confectioner's) sugar mixture, sifted
2 tablespoons boiling water
2 teaspoons lemon juice

Make the basic brioche dough, following steps 1, 2 and 3, adding the rind with the milk at step 1. Divide dough into 6 equal-size balls and knead on a lightly floured surface until smooth. Place in a 6 x 1 cup-capacity (250ml) lightly greased muffin tin. Cover with a clean, damp cloth and set aside for 1 hour or until doubled in size.

Preheat oven to 200°C (400°F). Brush the dough with egg and bake for 15–17 minutes or until golden. Cool on a wire rack.

To make the lemon icing, place the icing sugar, water and lemon juice in a bowl and mix to combine. Place the rack of brioche over a baking tray lined with non-stick baking paper and spoon over the icing. Allow to set and top with orange zest to serve. *Makes 6.*

chocolate-swirl brioche

1 x quantity basic brioche dough (see recipe, page 96)
75g dark chocolate, chopped
¼ cup (60ml) single (pouring) cream
1 egg, lightly beaten

Make the basic brioche dough, following steps 1, 2 and 3. Place the chocolate and cream in a small saucepan over low heat and stir for 2–3 minutes or until melted and smooth. Set aside to cool completely. Roll the dough out on a lightly floured surface to a 45cm x 30cm rectangle. Spread the dough with the chocolate mixture and, starting from the longest edge, roll to enclose the filling. Place in a 22cm lightly greased Bundt tin. Cover with a clean, damp cloth and set aside for 1 hour or until doubled in size.

   Preheat oven to 180°C (350°F). Brush the dough with egg and bake for 35–40 minutes or until golden. *Serves 8–10.*

raspberry and almond brioche tarts

1 x quantity basic brioche dough (see recipe, page 96)
50g butter, melted
¼ cup (55g) caster (superfine) sugar
1 egg, lightly beaten
½ cup (60g) almond meal (ground almonds)*
1 tablespoon plain (all-purpose) flour
125g fresh raspberries
1 egg, extra, lightly beaten

Make the basic brioche dough, following steps 1, 2 and 3. Roll the dough out on a lightly floured surface to 1cm thick. Using a 10cm round cookie cutter, cut 6 x 10cm rounds from the dough. Using a 7cm round cookie cutter, press lightly into the dough rounds to create a border. Place rounds on a baking tray lined with non-stick baking paper. Place the butter, sugar, egg, almond meal and flour in a bowl and mix to combine. Add the raspberries and spoon mixture into the centre of the rounds. Cover with a clean, damp cloth and set aside for 1 hour or until doubled in size.

   Preheat oven to 180°C (350°F). Brush edges with extra egg and bake for 17–19 minutes or until golden. *Makes 6.*

desserts

pavlova

panna cotta

baked custard

lemon curd

apple + blueberry crumble

soufflé

crème brûlée

baked cheesecake

crème caramel

pavlova

With its crisp sugary shell, soft marshmallowy centre and generous crown of cream and summer fruit, it's easy to see why more than one country lays claim to this classic dessert!

basic pavlova

150ml eggwhite (approximately 4 eggs)
1 cup (220g) caster (superfine) sugar
2 tablespoons cornflour (cornstarch), sifted
2 teaspoons white vinegar
1 cup (250ml) single (pouring) cream
½ cup passionfruit pulp (approximately 4 passionfruit)
250g strawberries, hulled and halved

step 1

step 2

step 1 Preheat oven to 150°C (300°F). Place the eggwhite in the bowl of an electric mixer and whisk until stiff peaks form.

step 2 Gradually add the sugar, whisking well, until the mixture is stiff and glossy. Add the cornflour and vinegar and whisk until just combined.

step 3 Shape the mixture into an 18cm round on a baking tray lined with non-stick baking paper. Reduce oven to 120°C (250°F) and bake for 1 hour 20 minutes.

Turn the oven off and allow the pavlova to cool completely in the oven.

step 4 Whisk the cream until soft peaks form. Spread over the pavlova, top with passionfruit and strawberries and serve immediately. *Serves 8–10.*

Tip: Use fresh room-temperature eggs because the eggwhite will trap more air and whip to a fuller volume.

cook's tips

beat – You can tell the meringue is stiff and glossy when the mixture has tripled in volume and stands up when the beaters are lifted out.

shape – For a perfectly round pavlova, trace the correct-size circle on a piece of non-stick baking paper. Place on the baking tray and pile the meringue into the circle. Shape with a palette knife.

almond pavlova stack

150ml eggwhite (approximately 4 eggs)
1 cup (220g) caster (superfine) sugar
2 tablespoons cornflour (cornstarch), sifted
2 teaspoons white vinegar
½ cup (40g) flaked almonds
1 cup (250ml) single (pouring) cream
2 peaches, sliced
¼ cup (60ml) dessert wine

Preheat oven to 150°C (300°F). Place the eggwhite in the bowl of an electric mixer and whisk until stiff peaks form. Gradually add the sugar, whisking well, until the mixture is stiff and glossy. Add the cornflour and vinegar and whisk until just combined. Shape the mixture into 2 x 18cm rounds on baking trays lined with non-stick baking paper and sprinkle with the almonds. Reduce oven to 120°C (250°F) and bake for 1 hour. Turn the oven off and allow the pavlovas to cool completely in the oven.

Whisk the cream until soft peaks form. Spread half over a pavlova, sandwich with the remaining pavlova and top with remaining cream. Place the peach and dessert wine in a bowl and toss to combine. Top the pavlova with the peach mixture and serve immediately. *Serves 8–10.*

rosewater pavlovas with blueberries

150ml eggwhite (approximately 4 eggs)
1 cup (220g) caster (superfine) sugar
2 tablespoons cornflour (cornstarch), sifted
2 teaspoons white vinegar
1 teaspoon rosewater*
1 cup (250ml) single (pouring) cream
300g blueberries

Preheat oven to 150°C (300°F). Place the eggwhite in the bowl of an electric mixer and whisk until stiff peaks form. Gradually add the sugar, whisking well, until the mixture is stiff and glossy. Add the cornflour, vinegar and rosewater and whisk until just combined. Shape the mixture into 16 x 8cm rounds on baking trays lined with non-stick baking paper. Reduce oven to 120°C (250°F) and bake for 35 minutes. Turn the oven off and allow the pavlova rounds to cool completely in the oven.

Whisk the cream until soft peaks form and serve with the pavlova rounds and blueberries. *Makes 16.*

chocolate and raspberry pavlovas

150ml eggwhite (approximately 4 eggs)
1 cup (220g) caster (superfine) sugar
2 tablespoons cornflour (cornstarch), sifted
2 teaspoons white vinegar
100g dark chocolate, melted
1 cup (250ml) single (pouring) cream
300g raspberries
icing (confectioner's) sugar, to dust

Preheat oven to 150°C (300°F). Place the eggwhite in the bowl of an electric mixer and whisk until stiff peaks form. Gradually add the sugar, whisking well, until the mixture is stiff and glossy. Add the cornflour and vinegar and whisk until just combined. Spoon ½ cupfuls (125ml) of the mixture onto baking trays lined with non-stick baking paper. Reduce oven to 120°C (250°F) and bake for 1 hour. Turn the oven off and allow the pavlovas to cool completely in the oven.

Dip the bases of the pavlovas in the melted chocolate, place on non-stick baking paper and set aside for 30 minutes or until the chocolate is set. Whisk the cream until soft peaks form. Spoon over the pavlovas, top with raspberries and dust with icing sugar. Serve immediately. *Makes 10.*

brown sugar cupcake pavlovas

150ml eggwhite (approximately 4 eggs)
1 cup (175g) brown sugar
2 tablespoons cornflour (cornstarch), sifted
2 teaspoons white vinegar
1 cup (250ml) double (thick) cream
orange-flavoured liqueur, to serve

Preheat oven to 150°C (300°F). Place the eggwhite in the bowl of an electric mixer and whisk until stiff peaks form. Gradually add the sugar, whisking well, until mixture is stiff and glossy. Add the cornflour and vinegar and whisk until just combined. Spoon into 12 x ½ cup-capacity (125ml) muffin tins lined with cupcake papers. Reduce oven to 120°C (250°F) and bake for 1 hour. Turn the oven off and allow the pavlovas to cool completely in the oven.

Carefully slice off the pavlova tops, fill with cream and sandwich with tops. Serve immediately with liqueur. *Makes 12.*
Tip: If you have an ice-cream scoop, use it to scoop the mixture into the cupcake papers for a lovely round shape.

almond pavlova stack

chocolate and raspberry pavlovas

rosewater pavlovas with blueberries

brown sugar cupcake pavlovas

panna cotta

Creamy, delicate and deliciously wobbly, this traditional
Italian dessert, meaning 'cooked cream', acts as a perfect
blank canvas for a multitude of flavour infusions.

step 2

step 3

basic vanilla bean panna cotta

2 tablespoons water
2 teaspoons gelatine powder
2 cups (500ml) single (pouring) cream
⅓ cup (55g) icing (confectioner's) sugar, sifted
1 vanilla bean, split and seeds scraped

step 1 Place the water in a bowl and
sprinkle over the gelatine. Set aside for
5 minutes or until the water is absorbed.

step 2 Place the cream, sugar, vanilla bean
and seeds in a saucepan over medium heat
and bring to the boil, stirring occasionally.
Add the gelatine and cook, stirring, for
1–2 minutes or until gelatine is dissolved.

step 3 Strain the mixture and pour into
4 x ½ cup-capacity (125ml) lightly greased
moulds. Refrigerate for 4–6 hours or until
firm. Remove the panna cotta from the
fridge 5 minutes before serving. Remove
from moulds carefully to serve. *Serves 4.*

*Tip: If the panna cotta is difficult to remove
from the mould, dip it into warm water and
gently shake to unmould.*

recipe notes

setting – The gelatine powder needs to be completely
integrated with the water before adding to the cream or the
panna cotta may not set. Sprinkle it evenly over cold water
and leave for 5 minutes or until the liquid is absorbed and
becomes firm.
size – To double the quantity of panna cotta, don't use twice
as much gelatine or you'll end up with rubber. You only need
1½ times the original quantity of gelatine.

passionfruit jelly panna cotta

2 tablespoons water
1 tablespoon gelatine powder
6 passionfruit, halved
½ cup (110g) white sugar
1¼ cups (310ml) water, extra
1 x quantity basic panna cotta (see recipe, page 106)

To make the jelly, place the water in a bowl and sprinkle over the gelatine. Set aside for 5 minutes or until the water is absorbed. Strain the passionfruit pulp through a fine sieve. You should have approximately ¼ cup (60ml) juice.

Place the passionfruit juice, sugar and extra water in a saucepan over medium heat and stir until the sugar is dissolved. Bring to the boil and simmer for 3 minutes. Add the gelatine mixture and cook, stirring, for 1–2 minutes or until the gelatine is dissolved. Divide the jelly mixture between 6 x ½ cup-capacity (125ml) lightly greased moulds. Place in the fridge until set.

Make the basic panna cotta. Allow the strained mixture to cool to room temperature before pouring over the firm passionfruit jelly. Refrigerate for 4 hours or until set. Remove the panna cotta from the fridge 5 minutes before serving. Remove from moulds to serve. *Serves 6.*

chocolate panna cotta

1 x quantity basic panna cotta (see recipe, page 106)
50g white chocolate, chopped
50g milk chocolate, chopped

Make the basic panna cotta. Once you've boiled the cream mixture, pour half into a clean saucepan. Add the white chocolate to one saucepan of the cream mixture and the milk chocolate to the other. Stir the mixtures until the chocolate is dissolved. Add half the gelatine mixture to each pan and cook, stirring, for 1–2 minutes or until the gelatine is dissolved. Strain both mixtures and set aside the white chocolate mixture.

Pour the milk chocolate mixture into 6 x ½ cup-capacity (125ml) lightly greased moulds. Place in the freezer for 20 minutes or until just firm. Pour over the white chocolate mixture and refrigerate for 4 hours or until firm. Remove the panna cotta from fridge 5 minutes before serving. Remove from moulds to serve. *Serves 6.*

brown sugar panna cotta with espresso syrup

2 tablespoons water
2 teaspoons gelatine powder
2 cups (500ml) single (pouring) cream
⅓ cup (60g) brown sugar
1 teaspoon vanilla extract
espresso syrup
¾ cup (180ml) espresso coffee
⅓ cup (75g) white sugar

To make the panna cotta, follow the basic recipe (page 106), substituting the icing sugar for brown sugar and the vanilla bean for vanilla extract.

To make the syrup, place the coffee and sugar in a small saucepan over medium heat and stir until the sugar is dissolved. Increase heat and bring to the boil for 5–8 minutes or until reduced and thickened. Refrigerate until cold.

Remove the panna cotta from the fridge 5 minutes before serving and remove from moulds. Pour over the syrup to serve. *Serves 4.*

cinnamon panna cotta with poached rhubarb

1 x quantity basic panna cotta (see recipe, page 106)
2 sticks cinnamon
poached rhubarb
2 cups (500ml) water
1 cup (220g) white sugar
3 x 5cm pieces orange zest
500g rhubarb, trimmed and cut into 8cm lengths

Make the panna cotta, adding the cinnamon to the cream and sugar mixture.

To make the poached rhubarb, place the water, sugar and orange zest in a large, deep-sided frying pan over medium heat and stir until the sugar is dissolved. Add the rhubarb and cook for 3–4 minutes or until just tender. Remove the rhubarb and set aside. Increase the heat to high and cook the syrup for 8–10 minutes or until reduced and thickened slightly. Refrigerate until cold.

Remove the panna cotta from the fridge 5 minutes before serving. Remove from moulds and serve with the poached rhubarb and syrup. *Serves 4.*

baked custard

A spoonful of this sweet childhood favourite is comforting and warm, like a hug. Create your very own bespoke custard by adding your favourite flavours to this classic recipe.

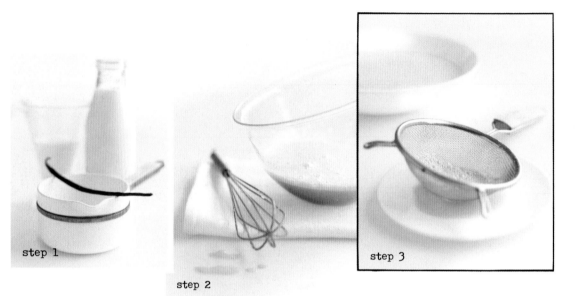

step 1

step 2

step 3

classic baked vanilla custard

2 cups (500ml) single (pouring) cream
1 cup (250ml) milk
1 vanilla bean, split and seeds scraped or
1 teaspoon vanilla extract
2 eggs and 3 egg yolks, extra
½ cup (110g) caster (superfine) sugar

step 1 Preheat oven to 150°C (300°F). Place the cream, milk, vanilla bean and seeds in a saucepan over high heat and cook until the mixture just comes to the boil. Remove from heat and set aside.

step 2 Place the eggs, extra yolks and sugar in a bowl and whisk until well combined. Gradually add the hot cream to the egg mixture, whisking well to combine.

step 3 Strain custard into a 1.5 litre-capacity (6 cup) ovenproof dish.

step 4 Place dish into a water bath (see cook's tips). Bake for 1 hour 25 minutes or until just set.

step 5 Remove from the water bath and allow to stand for 15 minutes before serving. Serves 4-6.

cook's tips

baking – Make a water bath by placing dishes in a baking dish lined with a folded tea towel and pour in enough boiling water to come halfway up the sides of the dishes.
mixing – By gradually adding the hot cream mixture to the egg mixture, **you will ensure the eggs don't scramble.**
heat – The custards should still have a slight wobble in the middle when you remove them from the oven, as they'll continue to cook from the residual heat on standing.

sugar and spice baked custards

baked lemon rice custard

marmalade brioche baked custard

baked chocolate custard cups

sugar and spice baked custards

2 cups (500ml) single (pouring) cream
1 cup (250ml) milk
1 vanilla bean, split and seeds scraped or 1 teaspoon vanilla extract
2 sticks cinnamon
2 star anise
¼ teaspoon mixed spice
2 eggs and 3 egg yolks, extra
½ cup (90g) brown sugar

Preheat oven to 150°C (300°F). Place the cream, milk, vanilla, cinnamon, star anise and mixed spice in a saucepan over high heat and cook until the mixture just comes to the boil. Remove from the heat and set aside.

Place the eggs, extra yolks and sugar in a bowl and whisk until well combined. Gradually add the hot cream mixture to the egg mixture, whisking well to combine. Strain into 4 x 1½ cup-capacity (375ml) ovenproof dishes. Place dishes into a water bath (see *cook's tips*, page 110). Bake for 55–60 minutes or until just set. Remove from the water bath and allow to stand for 15 minutes before serving. *Serves 4.*

marmalade brioche baked custard

360g brioche, sliced
butter, softened, for spreading
1 cup (340g) orange marmalade
1 litre (4 cups) single (pouring) cream
2 cups (500ml) milk
1 vanilla bean, split and seeds scraped or 1 teaspoon vanilla extract
4 eggs and 6 egg yolks, extra
1 cup (220g) caster (superfine) sugar
Demerara sugar*, for sprinkling

Preheat oven to 150°C (300°F). Spread the brioche with butter and marmalade and arrange, upright, in a 3 litre-capacity (12 cup) ovenproof dish. Place the cream, milk and vanilla in a saucepan over high heat and cook until the mixture just comes to the boil. Remove from the heat and set aside.

Place the eggs, extra yolks and sugar in a bowl and whisk until well combined. Gradually add the hot cream mixture to the egg mixture, whisking well to combine. Strain custard over the brioche and sprinkle with Demerara sugar. Place dish into a water bath (see *cook's tips*, page 110). Bake for 65–70 minutes or until just set. Remove from water bath and allow to stand for 15 minutes before serving. *Serves 6–8.*

baked lemon rice custard

2 cups (500ml) single (pouring) cream
1 cup (250ml) milk
1 vanilla bean, split and seeds scraped or 1 teaspoon vanilla extract
1 tablespoon shredded lemon zest
2 eggs and 3 egg yolks, extra
½ cup (110g) caster (superfine) sugar
1 cup cooked arborio rice**
¼ cup (40g) currants
finely grated nutmeg, to serve

Preheat oven to 150°C (300°F). Place the cream, milk, vanilla and lemon in a saucepan over high heat and cook until the mixture just comes to the boil. Remove from the heat and set aside.

Place the eggs, extra yolks and sugar in a bowl and whisk until well combined. Gradually add the hot cream mixture to the egg mixture, whisking well to combine. Spread the rice and currants over the base of a 1.5 litre-capacity (6 cup) ovenproof dish. Strain the custard over the rice and place into a water bath (see *cook's tips*, page 110). Bake for 50–60 minutes or until just set. Remove from the water bath, sprinkle with nutmeg and allow to stand for 15 minutes before serving. *Serves 4–6.*
+ ⅓ cup uncooked arborio rice will yield 1 cup cooked rice.

baked chocolate custard cups

2 cups (500ml) single (pouring) cream
1 cup (250ml) milk
1 vanilla bean, split and seeds scraped or 1 teaspoon vanilla extract
150g dark chocolate, finely chopped
2 eggs and 3 egg yolks, extra
½ cup (110g) caster (superfine) sugar

Preheat oven to 150°C (300°F). Place the cream, milk, vanilla and chocolate in a saucepan over high heat and stir to melt the chocolate. Cook until the mixture just comes to the boil. Remove from heat and set aside.

Place the eggs, extra yolks and sugar in a bowl and whisk until well combined. Gradually add the hot cream mixture to the egg mixture, whisking well to combine. Strain into 6 x 1 cup-capacity (250ml) teacups. Place teacups into a water bath (see *cook's tips*, page 110). Bake for 45 minutes or until just set. Remove from the water bath and allow to stand for 15 minutes before serving. *Serves 6.*
Tip: This recipe is also delicious served chilled. Simply refrigerate until cold before serving.

lemon curd

Sweet and buttery with a tasty tang, this versatile curd is a great stand-by for quick desserts, as a filling for cupcakes or cakes, and makes a great spread, too.

step 1

step 2

lemon curd

180g butter
¾ cup (165g) caster (superfine) sugar
⅔ cup (160ml) lemon juice, strained
3 eggs

cook's tip

To prevent the eggs from curdling in the hot lemon mixture, have them at room temperature before using. If it does curdle, press it through a sieve and return to the pan.

step 1 Place the butter, sugar and lemon juice in a saucepan over low heat and stir until the butter is melted and the sugar is dissolved.

step 2 Remove from the heat and whisk in the eggs. Return to heat and cook, stirring continuously, for 8–10 minutes or until thickened. *Makes 2 cups (500ml).*

try this...

SPREAD IT ROUND
Lemon curd is delicious spread over thick slices of toasted white bread for breakfast or even served with fresh-baked scones or pikelets and double (thick) cream for a dainty afternoon tea.

AS A FILLING
Lemon curd can be used to fill biscuits, a layered sponge cake or decorate butterfly cakes. Or use it to fill store-bought tart cases and top with cream for a cheat's dessert.

apple and blueberry crumble

1.2kg Granny Smith (green) apples, cored and chopped
1 cup (150g) fresh blueberries
⅓ cup (75g) white sugar
1 teaspoon finely grated lemon rind
2 teaspoons lemon juice
topping
1 cup (90g) rolled oats
½ cup (90g) brown sugar
¼ cup (35g) plain (all-purpose) flour
75g butter, softened
½ teaspoon ground cinnamon

step 1 Preheat oven to 180°C (350°F). Place the apple, blueberries, sugar, lemon rind and lemon juice in a bowl and stir to combine. Place in a large, ovenproof dish and set aside.

step 2 To make the topping, place the oats, sugar, flour, butter and cinnamon in a bowl and mix to combine. Spoon the crumble topping over the fruit and bake for 55 minutes or until the topping is dark golden and the apple is soft. Serve with double (thick) cream or ice-cream, if desired. *Serves 4.*

try this...

TOPPINGS

You can use different ingredients to create different textures and flavours. Rolled oats give toppings a rough biscuit texture and crunch, while a flour, butter and sugar mixture makes a fine-textured, cakey crumble. You can also use chopped, roasted hazelnuts for a nutty crunch and shredded coconut for a golden brown colour and delicious tropical touch.

FRUIT FILLINGS

Try making your crumble using your favourite fruits. Rhubarb and apple is a classic crumble filling, as is peach and vanilla. Most summer stonefruits make great crumbles and you can also add a selection of berries, such as blackberries and raspberries.

step 1   step 2

soufflé

End your meal on a high note with a perfectly risen,
light-as-air soufflé. Follow our steps and tips for
a heavenly and impressive result evey time.

basic lemon soufflé

⅔ cup (150g) caster (superfine) sugar
2 tablespoons water
2 teaspoons cornflour (cornstarch)
100ml lemon juice
5 eggwhites
1½ tablespoons caster (superfine) sugar,
extra
50g butter, melted
caster (superfine) sugar, for dusting

step 1

step 2

step 1 Preheat oven to 180°C (350°F).
Place the sugar and water in a small
saucepan over low heat and stir until the
sugar is dissolved, brushing down any sugar
crystals from the sides of the pan using a wet
pastry brush. Combine the cornflour and
lemon juice. Add the lemon mixture to the
sugar syrup, increase heat to high and bring
to the boil, stirring until thickened slightly.
Remove from the heat and cool slightly.

step 2 Whisk the eggwhites until soft
peaks form. Gradually add the extra sugar
and whisk until stiff peaks form. Fold
through the lemon sugar syrup. Brush
4 x 1¼ cup-capacity (310ml) straight-sided
dishes with the butter and dust with sugar.
Spoon the mixture into the dishes until
three-quarters full, place on a baking tray
and bake for 12 minutes or until risen and
golden. Serve immediately. *Makes 4.*

cook's tips

beating - Use a hand-held electric mixer to beat the eggwhites
until soft peaks appear. Gradually add the sugar and beat
until firm peaks remain when you take the beaters out.
mixture - Don't overbeat the mixture, or it will be grainy.
timing - After folding through the sugar syrup, don't let
the mixture stand, or the syrup and eggwhites will separate.

chocolate soufflé

⅔ cup (150g) caster (superfine) sugar
3 tablespoons water
½ cup (50g) cocoa, sifted
5 eggwhites
1½ tablespoons caster (superfine) sugar, extra
50g butter, melted
caster (superfine) sugar, for dusting

Preheat oven to 180°C (350°F). Place the sugar and water in a small saucepan over low heat and stir until the sugar is dissolved, brushing down any sugar crystals from the sides of the pan.

Add the cocoa to the sugar syrup and whisk to combine. Remove from the heat and cool slightly. Whisk the eggwhites until soft peaks form. Gradually add the extra sugar and whisk until stiff peaks form. Fold through the cocoa sugar syrup. Brush a 1 litre-capacity (4-cup) straight-sided dish with the butter and dust with the sugar. Spoon the soufflé mixture into the dish until ¾ full. Wrap a collar of baking paper around the dish so that it stands 2cm above the rim of the dish and secure with kitchen string. Place the dish on a baking tray and cook for 12 minutes or until risen and golden. Serve immediately. *Serves 6.*

raspberry soufflé

300g frozen raspberries, defrosted
⅔ cup (150g) caster (superfine) sugar
2 tablespoons water
1 teaspoon finely grated lemon rind
2 teaspoons cornflour (cornstarch)
5 eggwhites
1½ tablespoons caster sugar (superfine), extra
50g butter, melted
caster (superfine) sugar, for dusting

Preheat oven to 180°C (350°F). Place the raspberries in a food processor, process until smooth and strain through a fine sieve. Place the sugar and water in a small saucepan over low heat and stir until the sugar is dissolved, brushing down any sugar crystals from the sides of the pan. Add the lemon rind and cornflour to the purée and stir until the cornflour is dissolved. Add the raspberry mixture to the sugar syrup, increase heat to high and bring to the boil, stirring until thickened slightly. Remove from the heat and cool slightly. Whisk the eggwhites until soft peaks form. Gradually add the extra sugar and whisk until stiff peaks form. Fold through the raspberry syrup. Brush 6 x ¾ cup-capacity (180ml) straight-sided dishes with the butter and dust with the sugar. Spoon the soufflé mixture into the dishes until ¾ full, place the dishes on a baking tray and bake for 12 minutes or until risen and golden. *Makes 6.*

passionfruit soufflé

⅔ cup (150g) caster (superfine) sugar
2 tablespoons water
2 teaspoons cornflour (cornstarch)
100ml passionfruit pulp
5 eggwhites
1½ tablespoons caster (superfine) sugar, extra
50g butter, melted
caster (superfine) sugar, for dusting

Preheat oven to 180°C (350°F). Place the sugar and water in a small saucepan over low heat and stir until the sugar is dissolved, brushing down any sugar crystals from the sides of the pan. Place the cornflour and passionfruit pulp in a bowl and stir until combined. Add the passionfruit mixture to the sugar syrup, increase heat to high and bring to the boil, stirring until thickened slightly. Remove from the heat and cool slightly.

Whisk the eggwhites until soft peaks form. Gradually add the extra sugar and whisk until stiff peaks form. Fold through the passionfruit syrup. Brush 4 x 1½ cup-capacity (375ml) straight-sided dishes with the butter and dust with the sugar. Spoon the soufflé mixture into the dishes until ¾ full, place on a baking tray and cook for 12 minutes or until risen and golden. Serve immediately. *Makes 4.*

orange soufflé

⅔ cup (150g) caster (superfine) sugar
2 tablespoons water
2 teaspoons cornflour (cornstarch)
⅓ cup (80ml) fresh orange juice, strained
1 tablespoon orange-flavoured liqueur
5 eggwhites
1½ tablespoons caster (superfine) sugar, extra
50g butter, melted
caster (superfine) sugar, for dusting

Preheat oven to 180°C (350°F). Place the sugar and water in a small saucepan over low heat and stir until the sugar is dissolved, brushing down any sugar crystals from the sides of the pan.

Place the cornflour, orange juice and liqueur in a bowl until well combined. Add the orange mixture to the sugar syrup, increase heat to high and bring to the boil, stirring until slightly thickened. Remove from the heat and cool slightly. Whisk the eggwhites until soft peaks form. Gradually add the extra sugar and whisk until stiff peaks form. Fold through the orange sugar syrup. Brush 6 x ¾ cup-capacity (180ml) straight-sided dishes with the butter and dust with the sugar. Spoon the soufflé mixture into the dishes until ¾ full, place the dishes on a baking tray and cook for 12 minutes or until risen and golden. *Makes 6.*

chocolate soufflé

passionfruit soufflé

raspberry soufflé

orange soufflé

crème brûlée

2 cups (500ml) single (pouring) cream
1 vanilla bean, split and seeds scraped
4 egg yolks
¼ cup (55g) caster (superfine) sugar
2 tablespoons caster (superfine) sugar, extra

step 1 Preheat oven to 160°C (325°F). Place the cream and vanilla in a small saucepan over low heat and cook gently until the mixture just comes to the boil. Remove from heat. Place the egg yolks and sugar in a bowl and whisk until thick and pale. Pour the warm cream mixture over the eggs and whisk to combine.

step 2 Return mixture to the saucepan and stir over low heat for 6–8 minutes or until the custard is thick enough to coat the back of a spoon. Pour custard into 4 x ¾ cup-capacity (180ml) ovenproof ramekins and place in a deep baking dish. Pour in enough water to come halfway up the sides of the ramekins. Bake for 25 minutes or until just set.

step 3 Remove the brûlées from the baking dish and refrigerate for 3 hours or until set. Sprinkle with extra sugar just before serving and caramelise with a small kitchen blow torch until a golden crust forms. *Makes 4.*

try this...
CHOCOLATE VERSION
Follow the basic recipe, reducing the quantity of cream to 1 cup (250ml) and adding ¾ cup (180ml) milk. Pour the custard mixture you have made at step 2 into 85g melted dark chocolate and mix to combine before continuing with the recipe.

WITH A HINT OF COFFEE
For this delicious variation, dissolve 1 tablespoon instant coffee in 1 teaspoon boiling water. Follow the basic recipe. Once you've made the custard at step 2, add the coffee mixture and stir to combine before continuing with the recipe.

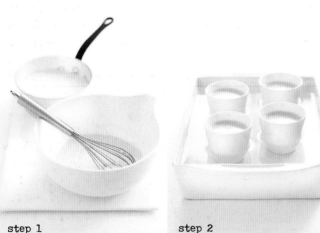

step 1   step 2

baked cheesecake

With its smooth richness and delicate flavour, this cake is a classic afternoon tea favourite. You can spike it with an array of flavours, from citrus to vanilla.

step 2   step 3

classic baked cheesecake

110g plain sweet biscuits
2/3 cup (80g) almond meal (ground almonds)*
60g butter, melted
filling
1½ tablespoons cornflour (cornstarch)
1½ tablespoons water
330g cream cheese, softened
460g ricotta
4 eggs
1⅓ cups (295g) caster (superfine) sugar
1 tablespoon finely grated lemon rind
¼ cup (60ml) lemon juice

step 1 To make the base, place the biscuits in the bowl of a food processor and process until finely crushed. Add the almond meal and butter and process until combined.

step 2 Press the biscuit mixture in a lightly greased 20cm springform cake tin lined with non-stick baking paper and refrigerate.

step 3 Preheat oven to 150°C (300°F). To make the filling, place the cornflour and water in a small bowl and mix until a smooth paste forms. Place the cream cheese in the bowl of a food processor and process until smooth. Add the cornflour mixture, ricotta, eggs, sugar, lemon rind and lemon juice and process until smooth. Pour the filling over the base and bake for 1 hour 10 minutes or until set. Refrigerate until cold. Serve with thick (double) cream, if desired. *Serves 8.*

try this...

You can substitute the lemon juice and rind for limes or oranges for a different flavour. Or omit the citrus completely and add the seeds of one vanilla bean for a creamy vanilla-scented treat. You can also sweeten the cake with honey instead of sugar.

recipe notes

You will need to use a springform tin to bake your cheesecake as, unlike other cakes, cheesecakes are fragile and can't simply be turned out to cool as they can crack easily.

crème caramel

This silken dessert can be both fresh and delicate
or wickedly rich depending on the flavours you add,
from seductive chocolate to tangy orange and more.

basic crème caramel

⅔ cup (150g) caster (superfine) sugar
⅓ cup (80ml) water
¾ cup (180ml) milk
¾ cup (180ml) single (pouring) cream
2 eggs
4 egg yolks, extra
⅓ cup (75g) caster (superfine) sugar, extra
2 teaspoons vanilla extract

step 1

step 4

step 1 Preheat oven to 150°C (300°F).
Place the sugar and water in a saucepan
over high heat and stir until the sugar is
dissolved. Bring to the boil and cook for
8–10 minutes or until the mixture is dark
golden. Pour into 4 x ¾ cup-capacity
(180ml) ovenproof dishes. Set aside for
5 minutes or until the caramel is set.

step 2 Place the milk and cream in a
saucepan over medium heat until it just
comes to the boil. Remove from heat.

step 3 Place the eggs, extra yolks, extra
sugar and vanilla in a bowl and whisk until
well combined. Gradually add the milk
mixture, whisking to combine.

step 4 Place dishes in a water bath (see
cook's tips). Strain the mixture and pour into
the dishes. Bake for 35 minutes or until set.
Remove from the dish and refrigerate for
2 hours or until cold. Remove the caramels
from the fridge 30 minutes before serving.
Turn out onto plates to serve. Serves 4.

cook's tips

baking – Make a water bath by placing dishes in a baking
dish lined with a folded tea towel and pour in enough
boiling water to come halfway up the sides of the dishes.
unmoulding – Dip the base of each dish in hot water for
10 seconds before turning out, helping the caramel slip
out more easily.

caramelised orange crème caramels

⅔ cup (150g) caster (superfine) sugar
⅓ cup (80ml) water
4 slices orange
¾ cup (180ml) milk
¾ cup (180ml) single (pouring) cream
2 tablespoons orange-flavoured liqueur
2 eggs, plus 4 egg yolks, extra
⅓ cup (75g) caster (superfine) sugar, extra
2 teaspoons vanilla extract

Preheat oven to 150°C (300°F). Place the sugar, water and orange slices in a saucepan over high heat and stir until sugar is dissolved. Bring to the boil and cook for 8–10 minutes or until mixture is dark golden. Carefully remove the orange slices and set aside. Pour the caramel into 4 x ¾ cup-capacity (180ml) ovenproof dishes. Set aside for 5 minutes or until the caramel is set. Place the orange slices on top of the set caramel.

Place the milk, cream and liqueur in a saucepan over medium heat and cook until it just comes to the boil. Remove from heat. Place eggs, extra yolks, extra sugar and vanilla in a bowl and whisk until well combined. Gradually add the milk mixture, whisking to combine. Strain and pour into the dishes. Place in a water bath (see *cook's tips*, page 122). Bake for 35 minutes or until set. Remove from the dish and refrigerate for 2 hours or until cold. Turn out to serve. *Serves 4.*

coffee crème caramel

1⅓ cups (295g) caster (superfine) sugar
⅔ cup (160ml) water
1½ cups (375ml) milk
1½ cups (375ml) single (pouring) cream
¼ cup (60ml) espresso coffee
2 tablespoons coffee-flavoured liqueur
4 eggs, plus 8 egg yolks, extra
⅔ cup (150g) caster (superfine) sugar, extra
1 tablespoon vanilla extract

Preheat oven to 150°C (300°F). Follow step 1 of the basic recipe (see page 122) to make the caramel. Pour into a 20cm-round cake tin. Set aside for 5 minutes or until the caramel is set.

Place the milk, cream, coffee and liqueur in a saucepan over medium heat and cook until it just comes to the boil. Remove from heat. Place the eggs, extra yolks, extra sugar and vanilla in a bowl and whisk until well combined. Gradually add the milk mixture, whisking to combine. Strain the mixture and pour into the tin. Place the tin in a water bath (see *cook's tips*, page 122). Bake for 40 minutes or until set. Remove from the dish and refrigerate for 4 hours or until cold. Turn out to serve. *Serves 8.*

whisky crème caramel

1⅓ cups (295g) caster (superfine) sugar
⅔ cup (160ml) water
1½ cups (375ml) milk
1½ cups (375ml) single (pouring) cream
⅓ cup (80ml) whisky
4 eggs, plus 8 egg yolks, extra
⅔ cup (150g) caster (superfine) sugar, extra
1 tablespoon vanilla extract

Preheat oven to 150°C (300°F). Follow step 1 of the basic recipe to make the caramel. Pour into a 20cm-square cake tin. Set aside for 5 minutes or until the caramel is set.

Place the milk, cream and whisky in a saucepan over medium heat until it just comes to the boil. Remove from heat. Place the eggs, extra yolks, extra sugar and vanilla in a bowl and whisk until well combined. Gradually add the milk mixture, whisking to combine. Strain the mixture and pour into the tin. Place tin in a water bath (see cook's tips, page 122). Bake for 40 minutes or until set. Remove from the dish and refrigerate for 4 hours or until cold. Turn out to serve. *Serves 8.*

chocolate crème caramels

½ cup (70g) roasted hazelnuts, chopped
1⅓ cups (295g) caster (superfine) sugar
⅔ cup (160ml) water
¾ cup (180ml) milk
¾ cup (180ml) single (pouring) cream
100g dark chocolate, chopped
2 eggs, plus 4 egg yolks, extra
⅓ cup (75g) caster (superfine) sugar, extra
2 teaspoons vanilla essence

Preheat oven to 150°C (300°F). Place the nuts on a small baking tray lined with non-stick baking paper. Place the sugar and water in a saucepan over high heat and stir until sugar is dissolved. Bring to the boil and cook for 10–12 minutes or until mixture is dark golden. Pour half the caramel over the nuts and pour remaining caramel into 4 shallow 1 cup-capacity (250ml) ovenproof dishes. Set aside for 5 minutes or until caramel is set.

Place milk, cream and chocolate in a saucepan over medium heat. Stir until chocolate is melted and mixture just comes to the boil. Remove from heat. Place eggs, extra yolks, extra sugar and vanilla in a bowl and whisk to combine. Gradually add the milk mixture, whisking to combine. Strain and pour into dishes. Place the dishes in a water bath (see cook's tips, page 122). Bake for 15 minutes or until set. Remove from the dish and refrigerate for 2 hours or until cold. Serve with the toffee pieces. *Serves 4.*

glossary +index

Most of the ingredients in this book are from supermarkets, but if you're unsure of an item, the glossary will help. We've also included a handy list of global measures and conversions as well as an index of all our recipes.

almond meal

Also known as ground almonds, almond meal is available from most supermarkets. Used instead of, or as well as, flour in cakes and desserts. Make your own by processing whole skinned almonds to a fine meal in a food processor or blender (125g almonds will give 1 cup almond meal). To remove the skins from almonds, soak in boiling water, then using your fingers, slip the skins off.

arborio rice

Risotto rice with a short, plump-looking grain. It has surface starch, which creates a cream with the stock when cooked to al dente. Arborio rice is available from supermarkets.

buckwheat flour

Buckwheat flour has a nutty flavour and is used to make Japanese soba noodles. It's also often used to replace regular flour. Unground buckwheat can be used as a substitute for rice. You can find buckwheat flour at health food stores and some supermarkets.

Chinese black vinegar

Used in stir-fries and other Chinese-style dishes, black vinegar is made from rice and has a rich and sticky consistency. There are many types of black vinegar, however Chinkiang (named after the Chinese province) is considered the best. It's available from the Asian section of the supermarket and Asian grocery stores.

Chinese cabbage

(wombok)

A versatile member of the brassica family, Chinese cabbage has a sweet flavour with a crisp texture. Although often used in Asian-style dishes, it can span an array of flavours and is delicious in salads and used to make coleslaws. You will find it at supermarkets, Asian grocery stores and farmers markets.

Chinese five-spice powder

This spice mix is widely used in Chinese cooking, the blend can vary, but usually consists of ground star anise, cloves, cinnamon, Szechuan (Sichuan) pepper and fennel seeds. Find it in the spice section of the supermarket.

Chinese rice wine

(Shaoxing)

Used for cooking, this low-alcohol wine is often added to stir-fries, marinades and sauces. Made from fermented rice and typically aged for 10 years, it has a similar flavour to dry sherry. Find it in the Asian aisle of the supermarket or Asian grocery stores.

crème fraîche

The slightly tangy and acidic flavour of crème fraîche is a result of cream undergoing a fermentation process. Originating in France, crème fraîche can be used in both sweet and savoury dishes and is similar in flavour to light sour cream. It's available from most supermarkets and specialty food stores.

Demerara sugar

Demerara is a raw sugar with large crystals. It has a rich, golden colour and an almost molasses-like flavour, which gives sweets an extra depth. You can find Demerara sugar in the baking section of the supermarket.

dry yeast

Yeast is a microscopic living fungus that produces carbon dioxide when mixed with water, flour and sugar. The carbon dioxide is what causes dough to rise. You can buy fresh or dry yeast; we use dry yeast as it keeps for longer and is readily available from supermarkets.

enoki mushrooms

These long, slender mushrooms with tiny caps can be added to Asian-style soups, salads and stir-fries. You can buy fresh or canned enoki, however, fresh is always preferred and will last in the fridge for up to one week.

eschalots

(French shallots)

These smaller-sized onions have a much sweeter flavour than regular onions and are delicious pickled, braised or roasted whole. They can also be chopped and added to sauces and salsas and are available from most supermarkets.

garlic chives

With a flavour that hints at mild garlic and chives, garlic chives are widely used in Asian cooking, such as in soups, dumplings and stir-fries. You can find them at some supermarkets and Asian grocery stores.

hoisin

This Chinese sauce is traditionally made from sweet potato, but is often made with fermented soya beans, garlic and chilli. It has a sweet and sticky flavour and is great in marinades or a dipping sauce. Find it in the Asian section of the supermarket.

horseradish

(grated and cream)

You can buy either grated horseradish or horseradish cream from the condiment section of the supermarket. It is delicious served with grilled meats and to give punch to meals. The pungent, peppery flavour of horseradish is more mild in the cream, while the grated horseradish is perfect for adding extra bite.

kaffir lime leaves

Dark-green and glossy fresh kaffir lime leaves are essential to East Asian cooking. Finely shredded and added to meals, they impart a vibrant, citrusy flavour. Find fresh kaffir lime leaves in the fresh food section of the supermarket.

lemongrass

An essential ingredient in Thai, Vietnamese and other Asian cooking, lemongrass has a wonderfully fragrant flavour and is easy to find in most supermarkets and Asian grocery stores. Be sure to peel away the tough outer layers of the citrus-flavoured lemongrass stalks before using.

Marsala

Marsala is a fortified wine originating from Marsala in Sicily, Italy. Its sweet flavour makes it the perfect accompaniment to desserts, such as tiramisu. Marsala is available from most good liquor stores.

mascarpone

This fresh Italian cream cheese can be used in a variety of sweet and savoury dishes. Find it in your local supermarket or Italian delicatessens.

miso paste

Miso paste is made from fermented soya beans and is used in many Japanese recipes, such as soups, and is often used as a marinade. You can buy red, yellow or white miso; red miso has a strong and salty flavour while white miso is more mild. The paste can be used for traditional miso soup but also makes a good marinade for fish, such as salmon.

OO flour

This is a superfine flour used to make brioche, pizza and some pastries. As OO flour is 'stronger' than plain (all-purpose) flour, it can withstand being stretched by a dough hook (giving brioche the right consistency). You'll find OO flour at supermarkets and food stores.

pancetta
(flat and rolled)

This Italian salt-cured pork belly is sold either rolled or flat in mild and spicy varieties. It can be used in the same way as prosciutto and is available from delicatessens and specialty food stores.

pickled ginger

Thin slices of ginger are pickled in a sugar and rice wine vinegar mixture. It has a sweet, fresh and gingery flavour and gives fresh bite to meals or can be eaten as a palate cleanser between courses. It's a common accompaniment to Japanese dishes such as sashimi. You will find pickled ginger in the Asian section of the supermarket or Asian grocery stores.

quince paste

Quince paste is often found served on a cheese platter, but also makes for a sweet glaze or sauce. Made from the quince fruit, the paste has a fruity flavour and slightly grainy texture that works well with rich meats and strong or creamy cheeses. Find quince paste in the refrigerated section of the supermarket or at grocery stores.

rice flour

Made from finely milled rice, rice flour is used to make vermicelli noodles and also gives a crispier texture than regular flour when used in baking, such as for shortbread. Find rice flour in the baking section of the supermarket.

rice paper rounds

Translucent rice paper rounds (or wrappers) are made from rice flour and are used to make spring rolls, Vietnamese rolls and wontons in Asian cooking. You will need to soak the rounds briefly in water to make them malleable and soft. They're available from Asian grocery stores and most supermarkets.

rice wine vinegar

Rice wine vinegar is simply rice wine that has fermented for longer, giving it a sharper, more acidic flavour. However, it still has a sweeter, more mild flavour than Western-style vinegars.

rosewater

With its distinctive floral taste, rosewater is a traditional flavouring in Middle Eastern sweets, such as Turkish delight. It's made by distilling rose petals and is also used in cosmetics. You can find rosewater in specialty food stores and Greek or Arabic grocery stores.

shrimp paste

A must-have ingredient for Asian recipes, shrimp paste is, as its name suggests, made from fermented, ground and sun-dried shrimp. It gives meals a depth of flavour and sweet aroma. You can buy shrimp paste in blocks or jars at Asian grocery stores.

smoked paprika

Paprika is a widely used spice made from ground capsicums (bell peppers) and a mixture of other flavours. The smoked variety is Spanish paprika (called Pimentón) and is available in three flavours: sweet (dulce), moderate or sweet and sour (agridulce) and spicy (picante). It adds a lovely smoky flavour and is a great rub for grilled or roasted meats.

Thai basil

Stronger and more peppery in flavour than regular basil, Thai basil is also distinguishable by its purplish tinge and longer leaves. It's a staple in Thai cooking and is available from Asian grocery stores and can sometimes be found in supermarkets.

turmeric

Sold either ground or fresh, turmeric is related to ginger and can be used in the same way. It will add colour and flavour to meals (not to mention your fingers and benchtops) and has a peppery, warm and slightly bitter flavour. Find it in the spice or fresh food section of your supermarket.

vermicelli noodles

These thin noodles are made from rice and need to be rehydrated in water before being added to salads, stir-fries and other dishes. They are readily available from supermarkets.

Vietnamese mint

The long, tapered leaves of Vietnamese mint have a peppery and minty flavour, making it a popular addition in Asian soups and stir-fries. Find it in Asian grocery stores and some supermarkets.

global measures

Measures vary from Europe to the US and even from Australia to NZ.

liquids & solids

Measuring cups and spoons and a set of scales are great assets in the kitchen.

made to measure

Equivalents for metric and imperial measures and ingredient names.

metric & imperial

Measuring cups and spoons may vary slightly from one country to another, but the difference is generally not sufficient to affect a recipe. All cup and spoon measures are level. An Australian measuring cup holds 250ml (8 fl oz).

One Australian metric teaspoon holds 5ml, one Australian tablespoon holds 20ml (4 teaspoons). However, in North America, New Zealand and the UK they use 15ml (3-teaspoon) tablespoons.

When measuring liquid ingredients remember that 1 American pint contains 500ml (16 fl oz), but 1 Imperial pint contains 600ml (20 fl oz).

When measuring dry ingredients, add the ingredient loosely to the cup and level with a knife. Don't tap or shake to compact the ingredient unless the recipe requests 'firmly packed'.

liquids

cup	metric	imperial
⅛ cup	30ml	1 fl oz
¼ cup	60ml	2 fl oz
⅓ cup	80ml	2½ fl oz
½ cup	125ml	4 fl oz
⅔ cup	160ml	5 fl oz
¾ cup	180ml	6 fl oz
1 cup	250ml	8 fl oz
2 cups	500ml	16 fl oz
2¼ cups	560ml	20 fl oz
4 cups	1 litre	32 fl oz

solids

metric	imperial
20g	½ oz
60g	2 oz
125g	4 oz
180g	6 oz
250g	8 oz
500g	16 oz (1lb)
1kg	32 oz (2lb)

millimetres to inches

metric	imperial
3mm	⅛ inch
6mm	¼ inch
1cm	½ inch
2.5cm	1 inch
5cm	2 inches
18cm	7 inches
20cm	8 inches
23cm	9 inches
25cm	10 inches
30cm	12 inches

ingredient equivalents

bicarbonate soda	baking soda
capsicum	bell pepper
caster sugar	superfine sugar
celeriac	celery root
chickpeas	garbanzos
coriander	cilantro
cos lettuce	romaine lettuce
cornflour	cornstarch
eggplant	aubergine
green onion	scallion
plain flour	all-purpose flour
rocket	arugula
self-raising flour	self-rising flour
snow pea	mange tout
zucchini	courgette

oven temperature

Setting the oven to the right temperature can be critical when making baked goods.

celsius to fahrenheit

celsius	fahrenheit
100°C	210°F
120°C	250°F
140°C	275°F
150°C	300°F
160°C	325°F
180°C	350°F
190°C	375°F
200°C	400°F
210°C	410°F
220°C	425°F

electric to gas

celsius	gas
110°C	¼
130°C	½
140°C	1
150°C	2
170°C	3
180°C	4
190°C	5
200°C	6
220°C	7
230°C	8
240°C	9
250°C	10

butter & eggs

Let fresh is best be your mantra when it comes to selecting dairy goods.

butter

For baking we generally use unsalted butter as it lends a sweeter flavour. Either way, the impact is minimal. One American stick of butter is 125g (4 oz).

eggs

Unless otherwise indicated we use large (60g) chicken eggs. To preserve freshness, store eggs in the refrigerator in the carton they are sold in. Use only the freshest eggs in recipes such as mayonnaise or dressings that use raw or barely cooked eggs. Be extra cautious if there is a salmonella problem in your community, particularly in food that is to be served to children, the elderly or pregnant women.

the basics

Here are some simple weight conversions for cups of common ingredients.

common ingredients

almond meal (ground almonds)
1 cup : 120g
brown sugar
1 cup : 175g
white sugar
1 cup : 220g
caster (superfine) sugar
1 cup : 220g
icing (confectioner's) sugar
1 cup : 160g
plain (all-purpose)
or self-raising
(self-rising) flour
1 cup : 150g
fresh breadcrumbs
1 cup : 70g
finely grated parmesan cheese
1 cup : 80g
uncooked rice
1 cup : 200g
cooked rice
1 cup : 165g
uncooked couscous
1 cup : 200g
cooked, shredded chicken, pork or beef
1 cup : 160g
olives
1 cup : 150g

a

aïoli 49
almond pavlova stack 104
apple and blueberry crumble 115
asparagus, potato and goat's
    cheese frittata 66

b

baked
    cheesecake 121
    chocolate custard cups 113
    gnocchi 41
    lemon rice custard 113
    marmalade brioche custard 113
    risotto 34
    sugar and spice custard 113
    vanilla custard 110
basil and lime beef rolls 63
beef
    carpaccio 56
    corned 16
    corned, in broth with salsa verde 18
    corned, hash 19
    corned, pies 19
    prosciutto-wrapped roast 15
    seared, with horseradish cream 58
    steak with chilli, lime and garlic butter 14
blini 55
blueberry muffins 94
brioche 96
brown sugar cupcake pavlovas 104
brown sugar panna cotta with
    espresso syrup 109

c

cake(s)
    baked cheese 121
    caramel and brown sugar sponge 76
    chocolate 79
    coffee sponge with mascarpone 76
    pound 78
    sponge 74
    vanilla cupcakes 85
caper and lemon butter snapper 33
caramel and brown sugar sponge cake 76
caramel slice 84

caramelised apple and pork terrines 52
caramelised eschalot and
    goat's cheese flatbread 71
caramelised orange crème caramels 124
chicken
    and creamy mushroom soup 25
    crispy skin, with creamed corn polenta 30
    and ginger soup with asian greens 25
    liver pâté 54
    and pistachio terrine 52
    and rice soup 25
    roast 20
    rolls, with chilli and coconut 63
    salad 27
    soup 22
    spice-roasted 21
    thai curry 47
    tomato and bean soup 25
chilli and anchovy flatbread 70
chilli and fennel roasted pork belly 13
chocolate
    cake 79
    crème caramels 125
    custard cups 113
    éclairs 92
    fudge icing 79
    ganache tart 83
    panna cotta 108
    and raspberry pavlovas 104
    soufflé 118
    sponge kisses, with strawberries 76
    swirl brioche 99
    swirl scone loaf 89
choux pastries 90
cinnamon
    brioche scrolls 98
    panna cotta, with poached rhubarb 109
    sugar puffs 92
classic baked vanilla custard 110
coconut
    chilli chicken rolls 63
    jam scones 89
    lemon curd tarts 82
coffee crème caramel 124
coffee sponge cakes with mascarpone 76
corned beef 16
corned beef in broth with salsa verde 19
corned beef hash 19
corned beef pies 19
country-style terrine 50
couscous 45

creamed corn polenta with
    crispy skin chicken 30
creamy mushroom and chicken soup 25
creamy mushroom gnocchi 41
crème brûlée 120
crème caramel 122
crispy skin chicken with creamed
    corn polenta 30

d

date and orange scones 89
dressings and sauces
    aïoli 49
    fresh tomato sauce 44
    gravy 48
    green curry paste 47
    onion relish 46
    vinegar and soy dipping sauce 60

f

fennel and coriander rolls 70
five-spice duck rolls 63
fish and seafood
    caper and lemon butter snapper 33
    kingfish, chilli and fennel carpaccio 58
    prawn, artichoke and lemon
        baked risotto 37
    salmon with miso dressing 59
    tuna with sesame and
        teriyaki dressing 59
flatbread dough 68
frangipane and lemon tart 82
fresh tomato sauce 44

g

garlic and rosemary oil flatbread 71
ginger chicken soup with asian greens 25
ginger pork parcels 63
grated zucchini frittata 66
gravy 48
green curry paste 47
grilled polenta with mushrooms and
    ricotta 30

bio

At the age of eight, Donna Hay skipped into a kitchen,
picked up a mixing bowl and never looked back.
She later moved to the world of magazine test kitchens
and publishing, where she established her trademark
style of simple, smart and seasonal recipes all
beautifully put together and photographed.

It is food for every cook, every food-lover, every day
and every occasion. Her unique style turned her into an
international food-publishing phenomenon as a best-selling
author of 19 cookbooks, publisher of the bi-monthly
donna hay magazine, weekly newspaper columnist, creator
of homewares and a food range, and shop owner of
the donna hay general store in Sydney, Australia.

Books by Donna Hay include: *fast, fresh, simple.,
Seasons, no time to cook, off the shelf, modern classics,
the instant cook, instant entertaining, the simple
essentials* collection and the *marie claire* cooking series.

www.donnahay.com

thank you

This book was put together in an extraordinarily short
amount of time by a very hardworking crew and I can't
thank them enough for their efforts. To designers Genevieve,
Hayley and Zoë for their clever design and layout. To Mel
and Lara for weaving their magic words. To Stevie, Kirsten,
Peta and Siobhan for re-testing some of these classics.
To William for his seamless new camera work in these pages.
Of course, this book wouldn't have come about if it wasn't
for the group of talented cooks, stylists, recipe writers
and photographers who have been working on the magazine
and the How To Cook columns over the past 10 years. Their
passion to bring you basic cooking techniques and solid
recipes is reflected in these pages. Bravo, team!